The Quest for Sustained Growth

The Quest for Sustained Growth

Southeast Asian and Southeast European Cases

Samuel F. Wells, Jr.
Barry M. Hager
Keith Crane
Paul Tibbitts
Karen Zietlow

WW Published by The Woodrow Wilson Center Press
Distributed by The Johns Hopkins University Press

Editorial offices:
Woodrow Wilson Center Press
One Woodrow Wilson Plaza
1300 Pennsylvania Avenue, NW
Washington, D.C. 20004-3027
Telephone 202-691-4010

Order from:
Johns Hopkins University Press
P.O. Box 50370
Baltimore, Maryland 21211
Telephone 1-800-537-5487

2 4 6 8 9 7 5 3 1

Library of Congress Cataloging-in-Publication Data applied for

ISBN 0-943875-94-3

ABOUT THE CENTER

The Center is the living memorial of the United States of America to the nation's twenty-eighth president, Woodrow Wilson. Congress established the Woodrow Wilson Center in 1968 as an international institute for advanced study, "symbolizing and strengthening the fruitful relationship between the world of learning and the world of public affairs." The Center opened in 1970 under its own board of trustees.

In all its activities the Woodrow Wilson Center is a nonprofit, nonpartisan organization, supported financially by annual appropriations from the Congress, and by the contributions of foundations, corporations, and individuals. Conclusions or opinions expressed in Center publications and programs are those of the authors and speakers and do not necessarily reflect the views of the Center staff, fellows, trustees, advisory groups, or any individuals or organizations that provide financial support to the Center.

Contents

Tables

Preface

This volume originated in a conference—sponsored by the Woodrow Wilson International Center for Scholars on September 17–18, 1998—entitled "Crisis and Transition: Southeast Asia, Southeast Europe, and the Global Economy." The idea for the conference developed out of the Center's Working Group on Global Capital, which had been meeting in confidential sessions since 1995 to examine the series of crises that had affected nations in Latin America, Asia, and Europe. The concept of the conference was to compare the strategies and mechanisms of the countries of Southeast Asia, which had had such great success but had recently experienced serious financial crises, with the slower and, in many ways, equally complicated transition from the command economies of the nations of Southeast Europe. The chapters that follow essentially provide a research report, with substantial additional statistical and analytical information, on the presentations at the conference. The final chapter updates more recent events and poses issues that remain as challenges for the international financial community.

This volume necessarily relates to some of the earlier discussions and analyses of our Working Group on Global Capital. These were very ably presented and analyzed in Barry M. Hager, *Limiting Risks and Sharing Losses in the Globalized Capital Market* (Woodrow Wilson Center Press, 1998).

I would like to take this opportunity to thank the group that planned the conference: Barry M. Hager, an attorney in Washington, D.C., who has been the guiding force of our Working Group on Global Capital at the Center; Warren Cohen, Consulting Director of the Asia Program; Li Zhao, Program Associate of the Asia Program; Robert Ponichtera, Research Associate of East European Studies; and John Lampe, Consulting Director of East European Studies. I should also thank our very efficient and energetic staff colleagues who helped with all of the arrangements and resolved all of the last-minute problems of hosting one of the first conferences to be held in the Wilson Center's new quarters in the Ronald Reagan Building. Our invaluable staff colleagues were Jane Mutnick, Margery Vaill, Kristin Hunter, and Aisha Haynes.

Samuel F. Wells, Jr.
Associate Director, Woodrow Wilson International Center for Scholars

Summary

Chapter 1 provides an introduction to this report, which summarizes the proceedings of a conference, "Crisis and Transition: Southeast Asia, Southeast Europe, and the Global Economy," held on September 17 and 18, 1998, and sponsored by the Woodrow Wilson International Center for Scholars. The conference assessed the recent economic experiences of these two regions, the difficulties they are encountering in generating strong and sustainable growth, the policies adopted by the governments to restore stable growth, and the role of international financial markets and international institutions in fostering recovery in these economies.

Chapter 2 presents background material for the overall discussion. It first provides a brief overview of all the economies in Southeast Europe. Subsequently, it reviews the transition from central planning to market economies and the stumbling blocks that Southeast Europe has encountered on this road. The chapter then presents a brief overview of the main economies in crisis in Southeast Asia. It concludes with a discussion of the key elements of the Southeast Asian crisis.

For the purposes of this conference, the participants focused on the countries that were in economic crisis in the two regions. For Southeast Asia, this included Hong Kong, Indonesia, Malaysia, the Philippines, Singapore, and Thailand. South Korea was added as a country not in the Southeast Asian region but as one having very similar problems that were dealt with in a comparable matter by the international financial institutions. For Southeast Europe, the conference organization included Albania, Bosnia-Herzegovina, Bulgaria, Croatia, Macedonia, Romania, Slovenia, and Yugoslavia.

Chapter 3 discusses the evolution of the recent crisis in Southeast Asia and examines the current state of the transition from central planning to market economies in Southeast Europe. It proceeds to evaluate the role that international capital markets played in the Southeast Asian debacle. It also analyzes the international community's dilemma concerning how to maximize the benefits of free-flowing international capital while minimizing the negative impact. The chapter concludes with a discussion of the challenge that the collapse in Southeast Asia poses to the "Washington Consensus," the package of policies—deregulation, privatization, trade liberalization, and free-flowing capital—that emerged during the years of British Prime Minister Margaret Thatcher and U.S. President Ronald Reagan.

Chapter 4 focuses on the constraints placed on central banks in managing economies in crisis or in transition. It discusses the benefits of and restrictions imposed by currency boards and other exchange-rate regimes on economic policymakers, using the example of Bulgaria. It also discusses the efficacy of conditionality, both in terms of policy and in terms of the creation or reform of institutions before the provision of financing to countries in crisis. The chapter also examines in detail how Indonesia fell victim to the "Asian flu" and why it was forced to look to the International Monetary Fund (IMF) for help. It explains why Indonesia was not able to credibly adopt a currency board whereas Bulgaria has found its currency board to be key to economic stabilization. The chapter concludes with a discussion of exchange-rate policy in Hong Kong and China and of the challenges facing the central banks in these economies to maintain current exchange-rate policies.

Chapter 5 assesses the banking sectors in the two regions. In light of the Asian crisis and the rocky transitions of several Southeast European countries, the creation of a strong banking sector is a significant prerequisite for long-term financial stability. This chapter examines the programs under way to help rebuild the Thai economy, with particular emphasis on the bank recapitalization scheme, and discusses how Slovenia has successfully worked through problems in its banking system.

Chapter 6 examines the effects of international capital flows and in particular the recent challenges, stemming from the Asian crisis, to parts of the "Washington Consensus." The chapter discusses the potential efficacy of placing limits on international capital flows. It evaluates the different approaches of Russia and Hungary to opening their markets to foreign capital and explains how structural reforms in the operation of the economy contributed to Hungary's greater success. The chapter then explains why Southeast Europe has had difficulty opening itself to international markets.

Chapter 7 summarizes the conference keynote speech, "Priorities of U.S. Policy and the Regional Role of International Financial Institutions," given by David Lipton, then Under Secretary for International Affairs, U.S. Treasury. The chapter discusses the changing role of international actors in maintaining global capital flows, noting the challenges to the "Washington Consensus." The chapter also analyzes possible changes in the operations, policies, and role of the IMF. Most conference participants argued that it is unrealistic to expect much more from the

IMF, either in terms of substantial additional funding or in terms of assistance in restructuring local industries and banking systems.

Chapter 8 summarizes the final conference session, which consisted of a roundtable discussion on world financial markets by four panelists: Jeffrey Shafer, Managing Director, Salomon Smith Barney; Jack Boorman, Director, Policy Development and Review, International Monetary Fund; Keun-Yung Lee, Chief Representative, Bank of Korea, Washington, D.C.; and Werner Schule, Counselor for Economic and Financial Affairs, Delegation of the European Commission, Washington, D.C. The chapter discusses the global nature of the current economic crisis and the role of global markets in triggering the crisis. The chapter examines potential ways of avoiding future crises and possible changes in the roles of international financial organizations. The session discussed the possibility of a transition from the current role of the IMF to the creation of a global bank supervisory authority.

Chapter 9 discusses key events that occurred after the conference, including approval by the U.S. Congress of increased funding for the IMF and the negotiation and subsequent adjustment of a financial rescue package for Brazil. The chapter identifies a range of unresolved issues that represent future challenges for the international financial community.

The Quest for Sustained Growth

Chapter 1

Introduction

Improving the material well-being of their citizens is the recognized economic goal of governments of all countries with market-based economies. Governments have attempted to pursue this goal by creating conditions that foster balanced economic growth.

Over the past three decades, many of the countries in Southeast Asia have enjoyed extraordinary growth in tandem with low rates of inflation, so much so that their performance has been characterized as the "Asian Economic Miracle." This happy period came to an abrupt end in 1997. In the course of a few short months, a collapse in confidence in Southeast Asian growth prospects and financial institutions resulted in successive runs on local currencies and a massive flight of capital from the region, precipitating deep economic recessions.

During the period of rapid economic growth in Southeast Asia, the countries of Southeast Europe were attempting to reconstruct market economies from the remnants of the socialist economies that had been created after World War II. In addition to the transition problems, many of these countries were embroiled in the Wars of the Yugoslav Succession or civil strife. Not surprisingly, economic growth in these countries has been elusive. Recovery has frequently been derailed by political or military conflict, balance-of-payments crises, or the collapse of domestic banking systems.

In both Southeast Europe and Southeast Asia, international financial institutions, most notably the International Monetary Fund (IMF) and the World Bank, have advocated rapid liberalization of goods markets, especially reductions in barriers to trade, tight fiscal and monetary policies, and stable exchange rates as prerequisites for economic growth. In addition, the U.S. government and the IMF have urged countries, especially in Southeast Asia, to liberalize capital markets. Once crisis hit in Southeast Asia, variants of these policies, that is, tighter monetary and fiscal policies, were advocated to stabilize local financial markets and eventually create the basis for economic recovery. This package of policies of opening domestic markets, freeing trade, and opening domestic capital markets to free movements of international capital have been labeled the "Washington Consensus." This set of policy prescriptions was strongly advocated by successive U.S. governments and the British

1

government under conservative governments throughout the 1980s and 1990s.

The ongoing problems of transition in Southeast Europe and the speed and depth of the declines in output in Southeast Asia have called into question the economic policies that have been pursued by these countries. In Southeast Europe, some local leaders have questioned the wisdom of rapid restructuring of large, state-owned industrial enterprises. Citizens and political leaders have worried about the economic and political repercussions of factory closures and large-scale redundancies. Both inside and outside Southeast Asia, a number of policymakers and economists are questioning the economic policies that were adopted, both during the period of economic growth and during the current crisis. They argue that risk and instability inhere in the reliance on external capital flows to fuel growth. Nations such as Indonesia and Thailand, which prospered based on the provision of capital by foreign investors, foundered badly as a consequence of global capital retreat.

Clearly, the Asian currency and financial crisis has had, and will continue to have, enormous international consequences. For the first half of 1998, there was hope that Asia's problems could be dealt with and that the region's economic difficulties would not spill over to other parts of the world. The events of late August and early September showed how vain those hopes were. The IMF's difficulties in coping with the problems in Asia, and now in other regions, raise serious questions about the ability of the international community to manage economic crisis. The turmoil in Asia, Russia, and now Latin America also raises fundamental questions about how, in an increasingly global economy, the developed world should assist the growth of emerging markets. These troubling developments form a world economic backdrop for the governments of other countries—such as those in Southeast Europe—committed to continued economic transition.

To examine these issues, the Woodrow Wilson International Center for Scholars sponsored a conference on September 17 and 18, 1998, "Crisis and Transition: Southeast Asia, Southeast Europe, and the Global Economy," which focused on the recent economic experiences of these two regions. Though different in many economic and political respects, the two regions plainly are engaged in the same pursuit of stable economic growth and just as plainly face parallel challenges arising from the current economic downturn.

The purpose of the conference was to compare the economic problems encountered by the governments of Southeast Asia and Southeast Europe and to explore potential policy solutions to achieve economic stability and resume growth. The conference compared the macroeconomic stabilization choices caused by the process of transition from centrally planned economies to market systems in Southeast Europe with the recent problems of macroeconomic stabilization in Southeast Asia. Although the sources of the recent economic crises in the two regions are different, countries in both regions are grappling with similar problems in creating a stable economic environment in which to resume growth. The conference also endeavored to determine the relevance of the Southeast Asian development model for Southeast Europe after the financial crisis in that part of the world. The conference organizers hoped that the comparison of economic developments in the two regions and the ensuing discussion would contribute to a better understanding of the problems of macroeconomic stabilization in these countries and would aid in the development of better policies for transcending the current crisis.

This report summarizes the discussion and findings of that conference and provides additional analysis of the key economic policy questions and answers that have emerged from the experiences of the two regions.

The opening session of the conference depicted the evolution of the crisis in Southeast Asia and examined the current situation in Southeast Europe. The participants examined both the origins of the crisis in Southeast Asia and the consequent challenges to the "Washington Consensus," suggesting that the dilemma for the international community is how to maximize the benefits of free-flowing international capital while minimizing its negative impact. The participants argued that the situation in Southeast Asia went wrong because the structures of free-market institutions in these emerging markets were not developed fully enough to face the rigors of the international capital and currency markets. Therefore, the international community should more clearly recognize that the creation of market regimes and institutions needs to be more advanced before emerging markets are subjected to the rigors of global capital and currency markets.

In Southeast Asia, development policies became imbalanced in the 1990s as governments attempted to maintain high growth rates, stable rates of exchange, and increasing flows of foreign investment while providing government guarantees to participants in poorly regulated financial markets. The result was a boom in real estate and securities markets, overvalued currencies, and increasing current account deficits. The last were financed by banks taking out short-term, foreign currency loans on the assumption that exchange rates would be stable and that governments would bail out the banks if they got into difficulty. In the spring of 1997, financial markets began to limit further access to credit as they questioned both the ability of countries to maintain sizable trade deficits and the worsening foreign debt-to-GDP ratios. To-gether, flawed economic fundamentals, poor economic policies, and structural weaknesses produced the 1997 currency and financial crisis. Conference participants also argued that the extended period of eco-nomic stagnation in Japan and the weakening position of the yen have been important factors in the Southeast Asian crisis as well. A number of participants also argued that the free flow, especially outflow, of international capital exacerbated the economic crisis.

On the most elemental level, the Asian crisis spread by undermining the confidence of the international financial community in these coun-tries. To sustain the mid-1990s high level of capital flows into emerg-ing markets, investors needed a high degree of confidence that the economies in Asia and elsewhere would continue to grow. Thailand's currency crisis in July 1997 caused second thoughts about other coun-tries in the region. Within months of the first signs of turmoil in Thai-land, dampened investor enthusiasm caused problems in Malaysia, Indonesia, the Philippines, and South Korea.

Financial markets have not been the only aspect to suffer an erosion of confidence. The events of the last fourteen months have implicitly challenged the "Washington Consensus," which emerged during the Thatcher and Reagan years, with its main tenets of deregulation, pri-vatization, trade liberalization, and free-flowing capital. The increasing attention given to slowing volatile capital flows by regulating them in some way has become an important challenge to the received wisdom of the last decade and a half.

In addition, the crisis has invited harsh criticism of the apparent inability of the IMF to cope with the crises. The dilemma for the inter-national community is how to maximize the benefits of capital avail-ability while minimizing the negative impact of free flows of capital through international markets. Clearly, there should be ways to encour-age longer-term debt and more foreign direct investment. The debates over capital flows and the IMF suggest the need for a review of the international economy's approach to financial transactions with emerg-ing markets. The decisions taken by and for Southeast Asia seem to have been wrong because the structures of the financial and economic institutions were not developed fully enough to face the rigors of inter-national capital and currency markets. Clearly, the Asian crisis illus-trates that in emerging markets, the capabilities of governments and private financial and business institutions are as important as the dis-cipline of the market.

The second session of the conference focused on the constraints on central banks in managing economies in crisis or in transition. In par-ticular, the benefits of and restrictions imposed by currency boards and other exchange-rate regimes were examined in detail. The session also dealt, explicitly and implicitly, with conditionality, both in terms of policy and in terms of the creation or reform of institutions before the provision of financing to countries in crisis. The session investigated the successes and failures of imposing conditions as part of macroeconomic stabilization programs and the institutional prerequisites needed to make such programs work.

In 1996 and 1997, Bulgaria experienced a collapse in confidence in its banking system and currency, spiraling inflation, and a sharp decline in output. The government, under the auspices of the IMF, responded to this state of affairs by adopting a currency board. The currency board has taken monetary policy out of the hands of the central bank; monetary sovereignty has been transferred abroad. The board is permitted to issue domestic currency at a fixed rate of exchange only if it possesses equivalent reserves of foreign exchange. In Bulgaria's case, the government chose a fixed rate of exchange of 1,000 leva against the deutsche mark. After the establishment of the currency board, the central bank no longer regulated the money supply; the money supply is now autonomously determined by the exogenous decisions of economic agents. The currency board was designed to overcome the deeply rooted reluctance to modernize the Bulgarian economy after seven years of piecemeal, inconsistent "reforms." It was also intended as a means to deal with the institutional failures of the first years of the transition.

The second part of this conference session explained how Indonesia fell victim to the "Asian flu" and why it was forced to look to the IMF for help. The session also discussed why Indonesia did not adopt a currency board. Lessons on how financial liberalization should proceed can be gleaned from Indonesia's recent difficulties. Since the 1970s, Indonesia worked to liberalize its capital account. Although currently many see only the negative aspects of these moves, capital account liberalization permitted Indonesia to grow rapidly during the subsequent years. However, the actions taken to open Indonesia to greater inflows of capital should have been complemented by additional policy changes, most notably closer supervision of the banking system and a concerted effort to reduce government influence on credit allocations. The Indonesian case demonstrates that there may be a need for greater administrative control over capital flows. Yet the session participants argued that capital account liberalization in Indonesia could not have been timed differently because the country needed the capital inflows to grow. Some lessons regarding financial liberalization can also be learned from the Indonesian liberalization process. Banking liberalization must be conducted in conjunction with an improvement in the financial infrastructure, including proper regulations and strict prudential measures, adequate disclosure, solid corporate governance, legal protection, and market discipline. The issue of central bank independence is also important.

The session also focused on the limitations faced by sovereign countries in the midst of an international rescue. This session demonstrated why a currency board was not an acceptable solution given Indonesia's circumstances, even though the idea was floated. Too many economic problems stood in the way of the institution of a currency board in Indonesia. The rupiah would have been strengthened if a currency board had been adopted, but little would have been done to improve confidence in the banking sector. Indonesian reserves were also unlikely to be substantial enough to support the base money required to run a currency board. As a result of crony capitalism and of individuals' close links with the government in Indonesia, the private sector was much more powerful than the state sector. A strong system of business ethics was also missing. Because of these economic weaknesses, a currency board would have been very difficult to implement and sustain.

Participants in this session discussed the commitment of the Hong Kong Monetary Authority and the People's Bank of China to fixed exchange rates. Some participants argued that these policies are not credible in the long run. Instead, given the particular circumstances of these countries, participants believe that the two authorities should choose new exchange-rate regimes, taking into consideration international market conditions, the degree of integration of each economy into the global economy, and the necessity of adjustment mechanisms against external shocks.

The third conference session dealt specifically with the banking sector. In light of the Asian crisis and the rocky transition experience of several Southeast European countries, the creation of a strong banking sector is a significant prerequisite for long-term financial stability. Financial crisis is always detrimental to economic performance, but the impact of the recent crisis has apparently been more severe in countries with weak banking structures and limited financial infrastructures than in countries with more sound foundations. This session examined the programs under way to help rebuild the Thai economy, with particular emphasis on the bank recapitalization scheme, and discussed how Slovenia has successfully worked through problems in its banking system. In general, the discussants argued that political pressures or implicit political guarantees contributed to the misallocation of credits. In addition to these problems, however, the banking systems also suffered from more traditional troubles. Both domestic and international investors fell victim to a certain degree of hubris. Share and property valuations rose very rapidly, and credit and investment decisions were made on the basis of these valuations. When values fell, banks found themselves with very large amounts of bad loans. To compound matters, assets and liabilities were mismatched: banks borrowed in foreign currencies and lent in domestic currencies, under the expectation that the exchange rates would remain fairly stable. The collapse of the exchange rates made it impossible for them to repay their foreign borrowings on the basis of revenues from domestic lending.

The next session of the conference centered on the topic of capital flows. As the global economic crisis widens, parts of the "Washington Consensus" are now being challenged. Most significantly, limits on capital flows are being considered in light of recent developments. There is substantial evidence that some fund managers, fully aware that Russia was headed for serious economic problems, moved money from Southeast Asia into Russia. Most fund managers assumed that Western governments and international financial institutions would bail out Russia and shield investors from losses. In fact, most investors have suffered considerable losses following the devaluation of the ruble. This devaluation and Russia's subsequent problems were due in part to its approach to international capital flows. Russia's government limited restructuring and favored shorter-term foreign portfolio investment. In contrast, Hungary pursued more extensive privatization and actively sought foreign direct investment. The two countries adopted different approaches to opening their markets to foreign capital. Hungary's greater success is due to structural reforms in the operation of the economy: the Hungarian government bankrupted loss-making firms, forcing them to restructure; the Russian government permitted loss-making companies to avoid making payments to suppliers and for taxes. Although the Russian government and central bank were successful in reducing inflation and maintaining exchange stability, the lack of structural reforms eventually led to economic collapse. Where portfolio investors went wrong was to confuse exchange-rate stability for structural reform. Because of the priority ascribed to low inflation and exchange stability by the IMF, any reworking of the "Washington Consensus" needs to take into account the difference between structural reforms and exchange-rate stability.

Southeast Europe has also had difficulty opening itself to international markets. Conference participants observed that because the European Union has conditioned further European integration for countries in Southeast Europe on more regional integration, the level and development of regional trade integration should become an important institutional and policy issue in Southeast Europe. However, there has been little regional integration thus far. The failure of these countries to integrate both regionally and globally has been an enormous loss to their potential development.

The final day of the conference began with a keynote speech by David Lipton, at that time Under Secretary for International Affairs with the U.S. Treasury. Mr. Lipton's speech, "Priorities of U.S. Policy and the Regional Role of International Financial Institutions," addressed the concerns about the risks of opening emerging markets to free flows of international capital and the economic costs to countries when capital flees. He argued that to some degree the current economic crisis in Southeast Asia reflects the economic and financial adolescence of these countries and is a stage that they need to move through. Weaknesses in domestic banking systems due to inappropriate investments and poorly matched assets and liabilities were the primary cause of the current crisis. With reliance on international capital to finance fiscal deficits, governments need to manage their budgets correctly. Because of pressures from international financial markets, the room for error in the construction of macroeconomic policy and debt management is very limited. Governments that overstep those margins invite trouble, as witnessed by the current problems of Russia and Ukraine. Mr. Lipton argued that the problem is not open capital markets but rather how those markets are managed. He also pointed out that international financial markets exacerbated the adjustment process because of the way in which local financial markets were opened and because of the failure of outside investors to act prudently. Mr. Lipton also argued that the IMF faces institutional and financial limits on what it can do. The IMF is owned by its members and works closely with them. The institution often does not feel comfortable going public with its misgivings about a country's problems, nor does it believe that such action would be useful, especially since by so doing, the IMF may precipitate the very crisis it is trying to prevent. Mr. Lipton argued that it is unrealistic to expect the IMF to be the principal whistle-blower concerning inappropriate economic policies. This job is more properly that of the rating agencies, who, in his view, failed to indicate the looming problems in Southeast Asia.

This session of the conference emphasized the changing role of international actors in maintaining global capital flows. It most directly debated the "Washington Consensus," and some participants concluded that in light of the Asian crisis, the tenets of the "Washington Consensus" may need to be challenged. In particular, two basic contentions emerging from the crisis need to be assessed: that free capital movements between countries are beneficial to the countries involved; and that the origins of the crisis lie in the free flow of capital. Some conference participants argued that the enemy is not openness itself but the way in which markets are opened. Furthermore, the opportunities created by openness are often misused. Although the benefits from the flow of international capital are enormous, openness must be dealt with in a way that minimizes the risk to the receiving country. The session concluded that to minimize the risks associated with inflows of portfolio investment from abroad, countries need to make changes in the operations of the national authorities, bank supervisory regimes, and the international organizations working in this area. In particular, national governments and banking regulators will need to be much more rigorous in supervising local banking systems. They may also need to better regulate the use of foreign loans for domestic lending in local currencies. Participants had few suggestions concerning changes in the operation of the IMF, however. Most participants argued that it is unrealistic to expect much more from the IMF, either in terms of substantial additional funding or in terms of assistance in restructuring local industries and banking systems.

The final conference session was a roundtable discussion on world financial markets by four participants: Jeffrey Shafer, Managing Director, Salomon Smith Barney, New York City; Jack Boorman, Director, Policy Development and Review, International Monetary Fund, Washington, D.C.; Keun-Yung Lee, Chief Representative, Bank of Korea, Washington, D.C.; and Werner Schule, Counselor for Economic and Financial Affairs, Delegation of the European Commission, Washington, D.C. Most of the panelists maintained that whereas the current economic crisis is global in scope, the crisis is not due to globalization. They argued that economic interlinkages have always existed and that the current problems have been caused by domestic instability. Mr. Lee took issue with some of these points. He argued that the depth of the current crisis is in part due to the rapid withdrawal of credit lines to Asian countries. This withdrawal precipitated much sharper declines in exchange rates than were warranted, and the sharp declines in exchange rates triggered the banking crises. He argued for better control of short-term capital flows in the future.

All the panel participants agreed that to avoid future crises, international financial organizations must learn how to exploit the efficiency gains that accrue from open international capital markets while they limit instability in world financial markets in the process of financial globalization. However, world financial markets are presently not well prepared to solve this problem, because they lack the stabilization measures available to national financial markets, most notably a true lender of last resort or a global bank supervisory authority. Because the IMF comes as close as any other institution to a world central bank, it must be provided with the resources to facilitate this stability in the midst of expanding globalization.

Chapter 2

The Crisis and Transition in
Southeast Europe and Southeast Asia

Although the core of this conference volume is the summary of the proceedings (Chapters 3–8), we have provided this chapter for readers who would like to refresh their memories concerning recent economic developments in the countries of Southeast Europe and in some of the countries in Southeast Asia. For easy reference, we have split this chapter into four sections. The first summarizes the economic and political history of the transition in Southeast Europe and the most recent economic successes and failures of these countries. The second describes the economic policies that international financial institutions and Western governments have encouraged the transition economies to adopt. The third section summarizes recent economic developments in Southeast Asia. We conclude with a brief description of the economic policies that international financial institutions have encouraged the Southeast Asian countries to undertake to end the crisis there.

Southeast Europe

For the purposes of the conference, Southeast Europe was defined as the countries of Albania, Bosnia-Herzegovina, Bulgaria, Croatia, Macedonia, Romania, Slovenia, and Yugoslavia, the last consisting of the republics of Montenegro and Serbia. The region is inhabited by 54 million people. Compared with the European Union, living standards are quite low. Albania is the poorest country in Europe; in 1998, per capita income was 1,428 1997 USD in purchasing power parity terms. Bosnia-Herzegovina, Macedonia, Montenegro, and Kosovo, the southernmost province of Serbia, can also be considered poor, especially by West European standards. The exceptions to this picture of regional poverty are Croatia and Slovenia. In 1998, Croatia and Slovenia registered per capita incomes of 8,530 1997 USD and 14,140 1997 USD, respectively, levels comparable with those of the lower-income members of the European Union.

The transition has been hard on all these economies. On average during the transition, gross domestic product (GDP) fell by a third in these countries from previous peak to trough; output in Yugoslavia halved. The fall in output in Bosnia-Herzegovina was even deeper because of the war in that country. Political instability and poorly designed macroeconomic stabilization policies were the primary reasons for sharper declines in output in Southeast Europe than in the Central European transition economies, but structural problems also contributed to the deeper declines in output. Industries in Southeast Europe, with the exception of those in Yugoslavia, were generally even more poorly adapted to the demands of market economies than were those in Central Europe. Because of earlier market reforms, some Yugoslav enterprises were directed more toward the competitive West European market than toward the less-demanding Soviet market. However, even in Yugoslavia, many enterprises, especially in the southern republics, have shown themselves to be uncompetitive in a market environment.

Educational levels are relatively high for countries with similar standards of living, although in the poorer countries, they are substantially lower than in Western Europe. A number of the countries have large rural populations: more than half the inhabitants of Albania and Romania live in the countryside, many of them engaged in subsistence farming. In most of these countries, large numbers of people are still employed by state-owned or formerly state-owned industrial enterprises that are often bankrupt. As the transition continues, many of these people will need to find new sources of employment.

Despite these similarities, the countries of Southeast Europe are a diverse lot. To better illustrate the problems they have faced in the transition and during the current period of economic turmoil in world capital markets, we provide a brief description of the economies of the countries listed above.

ALBANIA

Albania started the transition with the lowest per capita income and most underdeveloped industrial base of all the European countries. Agriculture currently accounts for almost two-thirds of GDP. Industry, on the other hand, accounts for a relatively small share of GDP, less than 12 percent, compared with well over 20 percent in other transition economies. Industry is heavily resource-based. Albania has large reserves of chromium, copper, and nickel and is among the three largest producers of chromium in the world. Albania's hydroelectric power is sufficient to provide most of its electricity. Consequently, the country is much less dependent on imported fuels than most other countries in the region.

Before January 1997, Albania was characterized as one of the model transition economies because of its rapid growth and its success in reducing inflation. Following a disastrous collapse between 1989 and

1992, Albania's economy grew 40 percent between 1993 and 1996. However, when a series of financial pyramid schemes fell apart in early 1997, approximately three-fourths of Albanians lost their entire savings. The ensuing protests turned into riots, and the central authorities lost control over much of the country. This period of anarchy created mayhem in the economy. After a rise of 8.2 percent in 1996, GDP fell an estimated 7 percent in 1997. Steady agricultural output saved GDP from falling further. After intervention by a foreign force led by the Italians in mid-1997, order was restored. The economy began a strong recovery in 1998, but growth in 1999 will be tempered by the Kosovo crisis.

Albania is the most ethnically homogeneous country in the Balkans: only 2 percent of its population consists of ethnic groups other than Albanians. The most prominent minority groups are Greeks and Serbs. Most Albanians are Muslim, although there is a large Roman Catholic minority. Clans continue to be of importance as many individuals maintain close ties to their villages or kinship groups. The population of Albania increased 10 percent in a matter of weeks as a result of the NATO bombing of Yugoslavia, with an estimated 400,000 refugees occupying camps in northern Albania as of May 1999. This humanitarian crisis would strain the resources of any country, but Albania is particularly ill-equipped to address the situation. Sympathy for Albania's humanitarian crisis will help facilitate foreign aid for the rebuilding of the Albanian economy. The IMF and the World Bank have already agreed to expand their aid packages for the country. The most important outcome of the crisis in Kosovo, however, will be an accelerated drive to integrate Albania more fully with the rest of Europe.

Albania remains NATO's staunchest ally in the region due to Albanians' feelings of solidarity with the Kosovar Albanians. Albanian leaders have condemned Serbian President Slobodan Milosevic and were among the first to call for an international armed response to his repression of Albanians in Kosovo. The government has nevertheless skillfully avoided fiery, nationalistic rhetoric that might exacerbate the situation. Even numerous Serb border incursions in the north did not draw Albania deeper into the conflict. Albania was largely willing to accept the heavy burdens caused by the inflow of refugees, but many Albanians expect significant monetary support from the West for their sacrifices.

BOSNIA-HERZEGOVINA

Bosnia-Herzegovina is a small, landlocked state inhabited by three dominant ethnic groups: Serbs, Croats, and a Serbo-Croatian-speaking group of Muslims. After Slovenia and Croatia seceded from Yugoslavia, the government of Bosnia-Herzegovina, dominated by the Muslim minority and with the support of the Croats, also seceded from Yugoslavia. Subsequently, war broke out, and Bosnia-Herzegovina became the scene of the most vicious ethnic conflict in the region.

Before independence, Bosnia-Herzegovina was in the middle of the former Yugoslav republics in terms of per capita income. The republic has a fair number of larger towns, such as Banja Luka, Mostar, Tuzla, Zenica, and Zvornik, which were home to large industrial plants that provided employment to substantial numbers of local inhabitants. Major industries included oil refining, ferrous and nonferrous metallurgy, electrical machinery, textiles and clothing, mining, and rubber products. In particular, the Yugoslav army had insisted on locating much of the country's armament industry in Bosnia-Herzegovina, since that republic was considered the most easily defensible because of its mountainous interior.

As a result of the Dayton Accords, Bosnia-Herzegovina has become a confederation composed of two equal parts: the Muslim-Croat Federation and Republika Srpska. The two parts have shown little inclination to cooperate with each other, and even the two parts of the Muslim-Croat Federation have difficulty getting along. Consequently, many major economic decisions are made at the subfederal level. However, a new currency, the convertible mark, which is tied to the deutsche mark, was introduced in 1998 and has begun to circulate more widely, especially since the Yugoslav dinar, which circulates in the Republika Srpska, has lost so much of its value. The Croatian kuna and deutsche mark are also heavily used.

Bosnia-Herzegovina has suffered the most severe decline in output of all Southeast European countries. According to the World Bank, by the end of the war in 1995, GDP had fallen 80 percent, to an estimated $2.0 billion from $10.7 billion in 1990. Due to a massive influx of economic aid and the end of hostilities, GDP surged 58.9 percent in 1996 and 52.0 percent in 1997. It is currently about $6.4 billion, roughly one-half of its peak. Because of the unequal distribution in aid, growth has been highly differentiated between the two republics. GDP in the Muslim-Croat Federation soared 53.3 percent in 1996 and 39.7 percent in 1997 while output in the Republika Srpska rose 74.5 percent in both years. Despite the high growth rates, economic development is disproportionately dependent on foreign aid from the United States and the European Union. Much of the increase in GDP is due to trade and construction; growth in industrial output and agriculture is only just beginning.

BULGARIA

Bulgaria's GDP fell 28 percent between 1988 and 1993. Growth resumed in 1994 and 1995, but then GDP fell sharply again in 1996 and 1997 as Bulgaria was engulfed by a balance-of-payments and fiscal crisis. The transition has been difficult for Bulgaria because, more than any of the other Balkan countries, it was dependent on the Council of Mutual Economic Assistance, the socialist version of the European Union, for its trade. Developing countries, particularly in the Arab world, were also of importance. Demand for Bulgarian products in both these markets fell sharply in the early 1990s, devastating Bulgaria's manufacturing industries. Because Bulgaria was primarily an agricultural country before World War II, many of its manufacturing industries were developed in the 1960s and 1970s on the basis of Soviet technologies. Few of these technologies, especially in machine building, have proved viable in a market environment; in general, enterprises have yet to restructure themselves. Bulgaria has also been burdened by a large foreign debt. The country borrowed heavily from Western banks in the 1980s. The funds were used for investment, were spent to finance Bulgarian exports to Middle Eastern countries, or were illicitly deposited abroad by Bulgarian leaders. The investments failed to generate exportable products, Syria and Iraq have defaulted on their debts to Bulgaria, and governments have been unable to track down capital sent abroad. Consequently, Bulgaria has been unable to meet debt-servicing schedules and has been through two debt reschedulings with both its commercial and its government lenders since 1990.

Although Bulgaria was encumbered at the start of the transition with a heavy external debt burden and a capital stock poorly designed to produce competitive goods for international or domestic markets, a major reason for its poor economic performance has been economic policy. Although Bulgaria made an excellent start in 1990 and 1991 under its first reform government, once this government was replaced by a weak coalition and then, from 1994 to 1997, by governments dominated by the former Communist Party, progress on reform was derailed. These governments failed to privatize and supported loss-making, state-owned enterprises through loans from state-controlled banks, which were, in turn, financed by the central bank. In some instances, managers funneled the proceeds from loans to offshore accounts. Consequently, progress on restructuring loss-making enterprises was slow, most major banks became insolvent, and there was little capital available for the private sector. The failure to privatize and endemic corruption deterred foreign investors. After declining for five years, Bulgaria's economy began recovering slowly in 1994, but a banking crisis led to a loss of confidence in the currency, resulting in a second severe recession in 1996 and 1997. The crisis was finally resolved through the introduction of an IMF-supported currency board in 1997. In 1998, GDP grew by 3.5 percent, and the economy is forecast to continue growing in 1999.

CROATIA

After Slovenia, Croatia has the highest per capita GDP in the region, at 8,530 1997 USD in 1998. Croatia's economy is fairly diverse. The country has an export-driven industrial sector and a very strong service sector. Tourism is a major force in the economy because of the attraction of the country's long, scenic coastline. For reasons of tax avoidance, large numbers of Croatian businesses are unregistered and operate in the "gray" or untaxed economy. This sector has been very dynamic; it is estimated at 25 percent of GDP and has been growing rapidly. Croatia has the geographical advantage of relative political and economic stability to its north.

Since 1994, Croatia has established a pattern of substantial increases in GDP in a low inflation environment. Croatia averaged annual GDP growth of 6.3 percent between 1994 and 1997, a growth rate that tops the region. GDP slowed to 2.5 percent in 1998. The central bank has done an excellent job in quelling inflation by adopting strict policies on releasing additional money into the financial system and by attempting to keep the value of the currency, the kuna, close to that of the deutsche mark. Although GDP growth has been strong, the price of the National Bank of Croatia's "hard" kuna policy has been stagnant merchandise exports and large current account deficits. Financial markets have become increasingly concerned about Croatia's ability to finance these large current account deficits. To compound matters, Croatia has favored "insider" privatization, the sale of assets at reduced prices to politically powerful elites, rather than sales of assets to foreigners. As a consequence, foreign investment has been limited. The combination of large current account deficits and limited foreign investment makes a devaluation and a resurgence in inflation a distinct possibility.

During the Bosnian war, the areas of Krajina and Eastern and Western Slavonia in which Croatia's ethnic Serbian minority was in the majority effectively seceded from the country and were nominally tied to the Republika Srpska in Bosnia-Herzegovina and Serbia proper. At the end of the war, large numbers of ethnic Serbs who had inhabited these areas fled the country; most of them have not yet returned. Consequently, Croatia's prewar population, which consisted of 78 percent Croats and 12 percent Serbs in 1991, has become much more heavily Croat.

MACEDONIA

Macedonia has the smallest population and the second-smallest economy in the region, after Albania. It is also the second-poorest country in the region, with a per capita GDP of only 3,040 1997 USD in 1998. Macedonia's economy is fairly diverse, with less than one-third of its economy dependent on industry and one-tenth on agriculture. However, some regions are completely dependent on the textile sector, which has faced difficult times.

After suffering from extraordinarily high rates of inflation between 1991 and 1994, Macedonia has effectively brought inflation under control with rates of 3.0 percent in 1996 and 4.4 percent in 1997. However, economic growth has been anemic. Although output did not decline as sharply as in other former Yugoslav republics, between 1994 and 1997 GDP stagnated. Growth is likely to remain modest until transport links with Western Europe are improved.

Macedonia has a large population of ethnic Albanians, roughly one-third of the total population. The government has attempted to maintain political harmony within the country. However, it has been hampered by uneasy relations with some of the country's neighbors. Bulgaria has considered Macedonian a dialect of Bulgarian and earlier this century thought of the area as a natural part of Bulgaria. Albania has been concerned about the treatment of its ethnic minority. However, the greatest difficulties have been with Greece, which imposed an embargo on the country for using the name of Macedonia, which is also used to denote a neighboring region in northern Greece. Because Macedonia is landlocked, the embargo imposed substantial economic hardships on the country, making a number of exports uncompetitive and sharply raising the cost of a number of key imports. The embargo has since been repealed, and Greece is now one of the largest foreign investors in Macedonia. Ironically, the crisis in Kosovo has led to improved relations between Macedonia, Bulgaria, and Albania as the countries have worked together to prevent the spread of hostilities.

ROMANIA

Romania is the largest country in the Balkans, with a population of 22.6 million, 89 percent of which is Romanian, most of whom are Romanian Orthodox (although in Transylvania, a large number are Uniate). Of the remaining ethnic groups, the Hungarian minority is the largest, about 10 percent of the total population. Romania is one of the poorest countries in Central and Eastern Europe, although per capita incomes are about average for the Balkans. In 1998, per capita GDP was 3,145 1997 USD in purchasing power parity terms. Industry accounts for one-third of the economy. The agricultural sector in Romania is much larger than in the other Balkan countries, excluding Albania, but no more efficient.

have been included in the first group of countries to be invited to negotiate accession to the European Union. Despite these strong positives, Slovenia does suffer from some transition ills. Because of the legacy of worker self-management, successive governments have had difficulty in agreeing on privatization. Ultimately, Slovenian governments have generally opted for employee buyouts; most companies have been purchased by groups of managers and other employees. This form of privatization has made it relatively difficult for foreign investors to take stakes in Slovenian firms. The relative lack of foreign investors appears to have kept the rate of technological change slower than in other transition economies. As a result, productivity and export growth has been less than in Hungary and Poland.

YUGOSLAVIA

Yugoslavia is composed of two republics: Serbia and Montenegro. Serbia has a population of 9.9 million people while Montenegro has a population of only 630,000, for a total population of nearly 10.6 million. Within Serbia there are three administrative divisions: Serbia proper, Vojvodina, and Kosovo, which respectively account for 59, 21, and 20 percent of Serbia's total population. Except for Bosnia-Herzegovina, former Yugoslavia, especially Serbia, is the most ethnically diverse state in the region. Less than two-thirds (63 percent) of the population is Serb. Albanians are the largest minority, accounting for over 16 percent of the population. They are largely concentrated in Kosovo, where they account for 90 percent of the local inhabitants. Hungarians are the fourth-largest minority, 3.3 percent of the total. They live almost exclusively in Vojvodina, where they make up 17 percent of the population. There is also a large Slavic Muslim population in Serbia proper and Montenegro. Due to the repressive policies of the current government and economic tensions, these ethnic splits have led to increased levels of interethnic conflict, especially between Serbs and Albanians. Kosovo is now wracked by war.

Yugoslavia is the most industrialized of the Balkan countries, with industry accounting for over half of GDP. The country also has a strong transport and communications sector due to its central geographical position in the Balkans. It is in the middle of the region in terms of per capita income. In 1998, per capita GDP was 3,000 1997 USD in purchasing power parity terms. After Bosnia-Herzegovina, the Yugoslav economy has been battered the most severely of all those in Southeast Europe. Between 1989 and 1994, GDP plummeted 51 percent. Many industries completely halted production in the mid-1990s as a result of the international trade embargo imposed on Yugoslavia because of its support for

Under socialism, Romania suffered under the most repressive gime in the region, after Albania. The leader of the country, Nic Ceaucescu, restricted contacts with the outside world and clam down on domestic dissent. His economic policies were focused on rapid development of heavy industry and machine building. After fall of Ceaucescu in 1989, Romania was ruled until late 1996 by for communists who were only hesitant reformers. Romania was one of slowest countries in the region to liberalize its economy. Privatiz proceeded very haltingly, and price and exchange-rate controls endemic. With the election of a noncommunist government in late economic policy has become much more market-oriented.

Similar to the output in the rest of the Balkans, economic ou declined sharply in Romania, by 30 percent through 1992. The econ began to recover in 1993. However, like Bulgaria, Romania plu into recession again in 1997. The failure to privatize led to conti large losses at state-owned industrial complexes. Inflation accele in 1996, and the exchange rate began to tumble. The new reform ernment elected in 1996 implemented an austerity program in 199 inflation was slow to come under control. GDP plummeted 6.6 pe in that year and fell 7.3 percent in 1998.

SLOVENIA

Slovenia, with a population of 1,991,200 people, is one of the sm countries in Southeast Europe; only Macedonia has a smaller po tion. It is also one of the most ethnically homogeneous. Slovenia h highest per capita income among the transition states; in 1998, pe ita income at purchasing power parity rates ran 14,140 1997 USD ing the post–World War II period, the country developed one of the advanced industrial sectors in the region and successfully expor Western Europe, although the former Soviet Union was also an in tant customer.

Slovenia was the first of the Yugoslav republics to secede. In 1 fought a short war with Yugoslav, primarily Serbian, forces, after the Yugoslav army left Slovenia. Subsequently, the country su from two years of high inflation. After introducing its new curren tolar, Slovenia quickly reduced inflation, which has been in singl its since 1995. Growth resumed in 1993 and has averaged a littl than 4 percent per year since. In contrast to most other states in S east Europe, Slovenia has run current account surpluses or very est deficits since the transition. Because of its solid macroeconomi formance, Slovenia is the only one of the Southeast European sta the Bosnian Serbs during the Bosnian war. Just as damaging to industry was the hyperinflation that struck the country in 1992 and 1993. Since 1994, GDP has risen sharply, up by an average of 5.3 percent per year, according to official statistics. However, the economy is still only 60 percent of its size in 1989. Despite favorable growth figures for the past few years, the basis for growth in Yugoslavia is flimsy. Much of the recent growth has been due to restarting production at plants that had been closed because of the embargo. Continued large increases in output will become more difficult because of the lack of investment in the country.

Within Yugoslavia, there are sharp regional variations in economic performance. Historically, the Vojvodina area has been the richest region in Serbia because of better infrastructure, higher educational levels, and rich agricultural land. In 1989, per capita incomes in Vojvodina were on a par with those of Croatia. Kosovo is the poorest Yugoslav region, with a per capita GDP only one-fourth of the country's average. Due to the armed conflict in Kosovo, industrial output in that region is at a standstill, particularly in the two largest sectors, energy and food processing. Serbia proper, especially Belgrade, has been hurt badly by the transition. Belgrade not only lost its position as capital of the much larger former Yugoslavia but also suffered from the collapse in trade relations among the republics, the move of financial institutions to the new republic capitals, and the sharp falls in transit traffic between the Middle East and Europe as a result of both the Iraqi and the Yugoslav embargoes. However, the region that suffered the most since 1989 has been Montenegro. Between 1987 and 1993, GDP there fell by two-thirds. Perhaps because of this experience, Montenegrins have elected a more reform-minded leadership than exists in Serbia. Its policies have contributed to faster economic development in Montenegro than in Serbia over the past few years.

Yugoslavia is the least reformed of all the economies in the region. Its economy remains largely unrestructured and several years behind Slovenia and Croatia in terms of implementing successful market reforms. The private sector's share of GDP was only 37 percent in 1997, the lowest share in the region. Under Milosevic, the current president, the government has fostered close links between enterprises, party officials, and the government. Milosevic's supporters control and in some cases own large stakes in major Yugoslav enterprises. Economic decisions are generally made in the interests of this group.

Kosovo has been occupied by a NATO-led, multinational peacekeeping force, suggesting a slow refugee return and Western aid channeled to Kosovo. Yugoslavia will be able to access some humanitarian aid and thereby support minor trade deficits. As long as Milosevic remains in power and Yugoslavia continues to pursue its socialist-era economic policies, however, more extensive aid will not be forthcoming. Yugoslavia will be in a semi-isolated state, whereby trade is allowed to resume but grows at a slow pace. The Yugoslav economy may experience a bit of a postwar bounce-back effect as capacity is brought back on line and the population focuses on the immediate needs of reconstruction. Beyond that, the prospects for medium-term economic growth and investment remain dim. The economy will run up against a wall of supply-side and labor-market rigidities, strangling growth. The inability to finance imports of crucial raw materials will have a further dampening effect on recovery and industrial growth. Wartime controls will most likely remain in effect for several months, easing slightly over time. Foreign investment, already thin in 1998, will be completely moribund. Monetary policy will continue to be relatively loose as Serb officials decide the key to pacifying the population will be to keep pension and other social-welfare payments flowing by printing lots of dinars. The gray economy, smuggling, and rent-seeking activities should flourish in this environment, especially as they offer the only real chance for most Serbs to make ends meet.

The Transition in Southeast Europe

In 1989, Bulgaria became a parliamentary democracy and began the process of changing its economic system from central planning to a market economy. In 1990, Albania and Romania followed in Bulgaria's footsteps. On a more sober note, former Yugoslavia fell apart in 1991. Five new countries emerged from the old: Bosnia-Herzegovina, Croatia, Macedonia, Slovenia, and rump Yugoslavia, composed of the republics of Montenegro and Serbia. These new governments not only had to oversee the process of creating market economies but also had to establish new states.

The steps involved in economic transition from centrally planned to market economies have been extensively researched over the past several years. A summary of the conventional wisdom on this subject was collected and summarized in a volume published by the World Bank in 1996, *From Plan to Market: World Development 1996*. Although the transition has been difficult in Southeast Europe, many of the governments in this region adopted the same policies to make the transition from plan to market as did other formerly socialist countries. These policies can be summarized as follows:

1. *Price Liberalization*. In all the Southeast European countries the new governments, by choice or default, have liberalized most prices,

permitting the development of markets. Under central planning, government officials played a major role in the allocation of goods and services, whereas markets played little role in determining who received what or what was to be produced. Once the new governments took power, they either purposely eliminated the planned allocation of goods and services or could no longer wield sufficient authority to channel resources. Consumer goods markets and subsequently producer goods markets emerged quickly, in most instances spontaneously. Prices in these markets are now set by market forces. However, in most cases in Southeast Europe, prices such as rents and utility tariffs continue to be controlled by governments. In general, these prices are still not set at levels that clear local markets or that permit producers to recover the full cost of production. Underpricing these goods has had severe efficiency costs for some countries.

2. *Lowering Barriers to Entry.* Before the transition, governments in the region severely restricted private-sector activity. In Romania, for example, private enterprises were virtually prohibited. Even in former Yugoslavia, the most economically liberal country, private businesses were constrained in terms of number of employees and revenues. Companies were not allowed to incorporate and were burdened with onerous taxes and licensing requirements. With the advent of new regimes, individuals were generally given the right to start their own businesses. Although bureaucracy and corruption often made creating a new business more difficult than in more established market economies, barriers to entry were sharply reduced when compared with the barriers in the former systems. Exit also became a fact of life for more firms. Private businesses had always faced "hard budget" constraints; if unable to pay their bills, private entrepreneurs went bankrupt. Under the new regime, state-owned enterprises also began to face financial restrictions. Most have generally not been closed, but the failure to make a profit has forced loss-making companies to reduce staff and other expenses and attempt to revamp product lines to increase sales. However, in Southeast Europe, governments have enforced bankruptcy laws for state-owned companies less rigorously than in Central Europe. As a consequence, restructuring has proceeded more slowly.

3. *Trade Liberalization.* Under the previous regimes, the countries controlled trade through state-trading companies or through strictures on currency convertibility. Imports were determined by government choice rather than market forces. Under the new regimes, pri-

vate companies and individuals are now permitted to engage in international trade. Traders now import goods demanded by domestic consumers and export products on which they can make a profit. The new governments not only have permitted companies to engage freely in international trade but have significantly lowered barriers to trade. Romania and Bulgaria joined the Central European Free Trade Association. Bulgaria, Macedonia, Romania, and Slovenia have signed various agreements with the European Union to liberalize trade. Because of the small size of these economies, gains from trade are extraordinarily important. In many instances, the countries do not produce particular products, or domestic substitutes are highly inadequate. Without trade, most markets in these countries would be bereft of competition, since there are only one or a handful of producers of a number of commodities. Reducing barriers to trade thus provides major gains in welfare.

4. *Currency Convertibility.* Trade liberalization has been possible only because the currencies have become much more convertible. In fact, as of 1998, only the Yugoslav dinar does not satisfy the IMF's definition of convertibility on the current account, that is, that residents and businesses are free to convert the domestic currency into foreign currency for the purpose of paying for goods and services purchased abroad or for making interest payments on foreign debts. Currency convertibility is a necessary condition for the creation of market economies; it is the means by which consumers are able to transform their domestic currency earnings into foreign exchange for the purchase of imports. Without convertibility, import competition for domestic products is severely reduced. Failure to permit convertibility results in very high opportunity costs, since trade without convertibility has to be channeled through state trading firms. Initially, currency convertibility was undertaken by permitting domestic companies and households to freely buy and sell foreign currencies. Exchange rates floated, depending on market forces. Subsequently, many Southeast European countries have adopted more controlled exchange-rate regimes. Some peg their currencies to a major foreign currency such as the U.S. dollar or the deutsche mark or a basket of such currencies. Others have adopted currency boards. Under a currency board, the exchange rate is fixed and the board is permitted to issue domestic currency only insofar as it possesses equivalent reserves of foreign exchange.

5. *Macroeconomic Stabilization.* The previous four policy measures are fairly easy to adopt. In all four instances, transition govern-

ments, either by design or by default, have ceased to try to derail or intervene in the operation of markets. Consequently, these measures can be implemented merely by eliminating past laws or regulations. However, eliminating hindrances to the free operation of markets has not been sufficient for successful transition. During periods of high inflation, markets generally function poorly; currency convertibility becomes difficult to maintain as households shift savings from domestic to foreign currencies. Not surprisingly, none of the transition economies have demonstrated an ability to generate sustainable growth without first reducing inflation to below 30 percent and then inducing continued declines. To reduce inflation to below these levels, all the governments have had some success through the imposition of tight monetary policies. For example, monetary policy (and the introduction of new currencies) permitted Yugoslavia and Croatia to conquer hyperinflation in a matter of weeks. However, as shown by the recent events in Russia, tight monetary policy is not a sufficient condition for other than short-term reductions in inflation. If investors lose confidence in the ability of the government to manage its finances, macroeconomic stabilization is endangered as investors, foreign and domestic, flee government debt markets and the local currency. In 1996 and 1997, both Bulgaria and Romania faced collapses in confidence similar to that in Russia in 1998 due to concerns about the banking systems and government budget deficits. Consequently, macroeconomic stabilization not only implies tight monetary policies but also involves the assertion of government control over its finances. For macroeconomic stabilization to take in the medium term, governments have to reduce budget deficits to manageable levels. When deficits have exceeded 4 to 5 percent of GDP for extended periods of time, the economies have generally suffered another bout of inflation and declining output as economic actors have lost confidence in the local currency. Many of the Southeast European governments have had difficulty in controlling budget deficits.

6. *Privatization.* The sixth policy measure necessary for transition is the privatization of most state-owned assets. Privatization increases economic efficiency, since private owners use capital and labor more productively and respond more quickly to market pressures as owners seek to generate profits. Although some state-owned enterprises have shown an ability to generate profits in a market environment, most large state-owned enterprises in Southeast Europe have not. These loss-making enterprises are funded

either directly from the budget, making it difficult for governments to restrict budget expenditures, or through loans from banks, which are often state-owned or state-controlled. When the loss-making enterprises reveal that they cannot repay these loans, the banks face insolvency. Not surprisingly, Southeast European governments have had to repeatedly bail out the banking systems because of bad loan portfolios. These bailouts result in increased government debt. In a number of instances, they have also resulted in sharp increases in the money supply and inflation as the central banks have pumped liquidity into the banking system. By privatizing state-owned enterprises, the governments increase the incentives of managers to reduce losses and eventually become creditworthy. Consequently, privatization is an important step for making it possible for the governments to control their budget deficits and avoid periodic banking crises as well as for increasing economic efficiency.

7. *Creation of an Institutional Framework for a Market Economy.* In addition to these economic policy changes, transition also demands the creation of the institutional framework needed for the operation of a market economy. Like privatization, the creation of economic institutions involves sustained government efforts. Legal codes need to be rewritten, regulatory institutions need to be set up, and government agencies—from statistical offices to tax-collection services—have to change their manner of operation. Like privatization, the creation of the needed institutional framework has yet to be completed by any transition economy, including those in Southeast Europe.

Although the governments of the Southeast European states have adopted many of these policies, the process of transition has been much rockier in this region than in Central Europe. Part of the difficulties they have encountered in the transition are due to more difficult starting conditions. The countries of Southeast Europe are in general located much farther from wealthy West European markets than are the Central European transition economies. The difference in geography has made the redirection of trade more difficult. In Bosnia-Herzegovina, war was the reason for the horrendous decline in real incomes. In other former Yugoslavia republics, hostilities and the collapse of internal markets contributed to falls in GDP of over 50 percent.

This said, ill-devised economic policies have been a key factor in poor economic performance. Southeast European governments have often been slower to deregulate prices, slower to lower barriers to entry and trade, and slower to make their currencies convertible than the Central European states. Albania, Bulgaria, Romania, and Yugoslavia have also performed much more poorly in terms of macroeconomic stabilization than have the Central European states, although Croatia, Macedonia, and Slovenia have had somewhat better records. None of the countries have attempted to privatize as aggressively as the Czech Republic and Hungary.

These policy failures have had economic costs. After sharp initial declines in output in Central Europe at the beginning of the transition, all of the Central European economies have experienced periods of strong growth and declining inflation. In Southeast Europe, the declines in output were much deeper and economic recovery has been much more erratic. Despite periods of economic growth, Albania, Bulgaria, and Romania have suffered sharp new recessions over the past few years because of economic mismanagement and political turmoil.

Initially, inflation rates were much higher in Southeast Europe than in the Central European transition economies. Early on, governments and central banks liberally printed money to cover budget deficits. These policies triggered true hyperinflation in Croatia and Yugoslavia. However, once governments and central banks implemented tight monetary policies, inflation rates in Croatia, Macedonia, and Slovenia fell below rates in Central Europe. Some governments have had difficulty sustaining lower inflation rates. In particular, low inflation rates have been very vulnerable to the health of the financial sector, fiscal discipline, and balance-of-payments pressures. Initial progress on inflation can quickly be reversed because of problems in these sectors. When Albania's financial sector collapsed in 1996 and 1997 due to the failure of a number of financial pyramid schemes (which were implicitly supported by the government), inflation surged. The resulting economic turmoil contributed to the disintegration of civil order and to a major international crisis. Although Albania is an extreme case, other governments in the region have also experienced a resurgence in inflation and another collapse in output.

The biggest threat to controlling inflation has been lack of fiscal discipline. This appears directly in large central government budget deficits, is hidden in off-budget accounts, or is disguised in government-directed loans through the banking system, which is usually state-controlled if not state-owned. The costs of subsidizing enterprises through the banking system can be enormous. In Bulgaria, inflation declined from a peak of 334 percent in 1991 to 62 percent in 1995. However, mounting bad debt problems in the banking sector due to loans to loss-making state-owned enterprises caused the banking system to collapse. As the central bank attempted to keep the banks afloat through injections of credits, inflation soared to 1,083 percent in 1997. Once monetary and fiscal discipline was restored through IMF pressure, inflation rates fell sharply.

Because these economies are so open to trade, the battle to keep inflation low also involves exchange-rate stability. Stable exchange rates provide a nominal anchor against which people can compare prices and wages. Such rates also help enterprises set prices and handle costs, especially important in small, open economies like those in Southeast Europe in which trade plays a very important role in providing markets and satisfying domestic demand. However, as in Southeast Asia, once exchange rates fall, inflation quickly surges.

Many Southeast European countries have struggled with exchange-rate policy. They have used a variety of exchange-rate regimes in an attempt to reduce inflation and maintain external balance. Albania, Croatia, and Macedonia, three of the most successful countries in terms of inflation, all ostensibly use floating rates. However, the floats are dirty; the three central banks intervene in the foreign-exchange markets, at times heavily. Romania also uses a floating rate but currently has had less success in reducing inflation than have these countries. The initial choice of a floating rate was dictated in part by the lack of foreign-exchange reserves in the coffers of the central banks at the beginning of the transition. Once foreign-exchange reserves rose, the governments sought to reduce exchange-rate volatility. At the other extreme, Bosnia-Herzegovina's new national currency, the convertible mark, introduced in May 1998, is operated by a currency board. Bulgaria's stabilization program, begun in 1997, has also included a currency board. Yugoslavia has used a quasi–currency board over the last few years, but the government has forced the central bank to repudiate the system when the government has run short of cash. Not surprisingly, inflation has surged following these episodes.

When national currencies become overvalued, they can also contribute to external disequilibrium as current account deficits expand and export growth slows. In Croatia, for example, the strong local currency has helped reduce inflation and stabilize the economy, but exports have stagnated or fallen over the past few years, and the current account deficit has widened.

Like their counterparts in Southeast Asia, the Southeast European economies have been highly susceptible to balance-of-payments pressures. Because of the relatively small size of these economies and the concomitant importance of trade flows for production and consumption, balance-of-payments disequilibria have major effects on aggregate output and demand. Not surprisingly, balance-of-payments and currency crises have often been the main culprit in derailing economic growth in these countries.

Early in the transition, many of the new countries had little or no access to foreign credits, so current account balances were positive out of necessity. A country cannot run a current account deficit if no outside investor is willing to finance it. However, in the ensuing years, current accounts have frequently gone heavily into deficit as opportunities to borrow or inflows of investment capital have made it possible for large increases in imports. The smaller countries have frequently had the largest swings in current accounts. Albania's current account balance went from a $14.7 million surplus in 1993 to a deficit of $276 million, nearly 12 percent of GDP in 1997. With the exceptions of Croatia, Romania, and Slovenia, the other countries have had little access to international capital markets to finance these deficits. Most of the deficits of the other countries have been financed by trade credits, loans from international financial institutions, and foreign-currency savings of local citizens; net inflows of foreign direct investment and portfolio capital remain negligible.

For some of the countries, the problems of transition and balance-of-payments pressures have been exacerbated by large foreign debts. All of the Yugoslav republics became independent with substantial debt burdens, which they chose not to service. The last restructuring of former Yugoslav debt included a provision that all republics would have joint responsibility for former Yugoslavia's total debt. After independence, the successor states repudiated the agreement. Since then, international commercial creditors have been engaged in debt negotiations to allocate and attempt to obtain repayment of this debt. The decisions to repudiate the debt had financial consequences. Croatia was excluded from international financial markets until 1996, when the London and Paris Clubs restructured Croatia's Yugoslav-era debt.

The country that has suffered the most from pretransition debts has been Bulgaria. Gross debt ran $12.3 billion in 1991 while exports were only $3.7 billion. The country was forced to declare a moratorium on debt repayments in that year. Negotiations on restructuring the debt ran until 1994, when the Paris and London Clubs signed rescheduling and debt-forgiveness agreements that forgave nearly $3.8 billion in debt. Due to economic mismanagement, the country abrogated this agreement in 1996, and a new agreement had to be worked out. The lengthy restructuring process has resulted in debt payments that are still quite large.

The other countries entered the transition with fairly low debt burdens but have had difficulty tapping international financial markets because of ongoing concerns by banks and other lenders about the ability of these countries to service additional debt. Because of these countries' lack of creditworthiness, international financial institutions and official and multilateral lending will continue to figure prominently in financing the needs of the Southeast European economies.

Southeast Asia

Southeast Asia encompasses the members of the Southeast Asia Economic Association (ASEAN) (Brunei, Indonesia, Malaysia, the Philippines, Singapore, Thailand, and Vietnam), Burma, Cambodia, and Laos. However, for the purposes of this conference, the participants focused on the "tiger economies" that have recently experienced economic crises: Hong Kong (now part of China), Indonesia, Malaysia, the Philippines, Singapore, and Thailand. In addition, the conference discussed the policies and problems of South Korea, a country that is not part of Southeast Asia but that has definitely been a "tiger" economy and ran into severe economic difficulties in 1997. Below we provide brief economic overviews of these countries.[1]

HONG KONG

No longer a colony and now technically part of China, Hong Kong is still treated as a separate economic entity because of China's agreement with Great Britain to keep two systems within one country. Hong Kong has enjoyed very strong economic growth for the past four decades. Per capita incomes at purchasing power parity rates hit 25,950 1997 USD in 1998; at market exchange rates, incomes ran $24,890, placing Hong Kong among the wealthiest countries in the world. As incomes have risen, GDP growth has slowed to more moderate rates than elsewhere in the region. Growth rates averaged 5 percent between 1993 and 1997.

Because of the increase in wages in Hong Kong, manufacturing has fled the city for the mainland. Hong Kong is now primarily a service economy, providing shipping, finance, and communications services for mainland China or businesses serving the mainland. The Hong Kong monetary authorities have pegged the Hong Kong dollar to the U.S. dollar. So far, the Hong Kong dollar has held, but it has periodically come under strong pressure to devalue since the Thai crisis of last year. The monetary authorities have raised interest rates and recently intervened on the Hong Kong stock market so as to defend the currency. In part because of high interest rates and the fall in the stock market, and in part because of the decline in economic activity throughout the region and a consequent slowdown in Chinese exports, Hong Kong fell into recession in the first part of 1998 due to the "Asian flu."

INDONESIA

Indonesia is the largest country in the region. Like the Philippines, it is an archipelago nation, composed of dozens of different ethnic and tribal groups. The country is home to 204.4 million people, most of them concentrated on the islands of Java, Bali, and Sumatra. Java and Bali are two of the most densely populated areas in the world. The dominant ethnic group is the Javanese, a Malay group that is primarily Muslim. The Chinese minority, about 1 percent of the population, is primarily Christian. Much of Indonesia's wealth is concentrated within this group, which has contributed to ethnic tensions. Indonesia is one of the poorest of the tigers; per capita incomes in purchasing power parity terms ran 3,450 1997 USD in 1998. Due to the very sharp decline in output triggered by the Asian crisis, per capita incomes fell sharply in 1998 and poverty rates have soared.

This poverty exists despite the fact that Indonesia reported very high growth rates in the 1980s and 1990s. Between 1994 and 1997, GDP growth averaged over 7 percent per year. The country has benefited from substantial exports of oil, gas, and lumber, but the increases in GDP in the 1980s and 1990s were triggered by explosive growth in manufacturing, much of it lower value-added products such as shoes and clothing for export. In 1996, before the devaluation, GDP ran $225.8 billion at market exchange rates. The current account deficit totaled 3.5 percent of GDP.

Indonesia has been hit very hard by the Asian crisis. Political power was concentrated in the hands of the former president Suharto. Although his economic policy team kept inflation low, the exchange rate stable, and the budget under control, the regime employed a variety of administrative controls to regulate the economy. Exports and imports of a number of important goods such as cloves, palm oil, and automobiles were regulated by government boards or licenses. These policies contributed to a high level of corruption, according to a number of observers. In addition, because of the importance of government awards or regulations for business ventures, political connections became of prime importance for the success of a business venture. Banks made loans on the basis of contract awards and government connections, not always on the basis of the creditworthiness of particular projects. To compound matters, the banking system was poorly supervised. A long period of a fixed exchange rate encouraged banks to borrow abroad in foreign currency and relend domestically in the local currency; positions were often unhedged, that is, the bankers failed to buy forward contracts insuring that repayments in rupiah would be adequate to repay their own loans in foreign currency. Consequently, when the Indonesian currency came under pressure following Thailand's problems, the devaluation of the currency precipitated a banking crisis. The subsequent economic turmoil contributed to the political unrest that resulted in Suharto's resignation in early 1998. Although Suharto's departure appears to have been a necessary condition for changing economic policy, the ensuing political instability, especially riots directed at Indonesia's Chinese minority, has resulted in the flight of capital and entrepreneurs from the country, intensifying the downturn. Standard & Poor's *DRI* now expects GDP to fall 5.3 percent in 1999 after a 15.1 percent decline in GDP in 1998.

MALAYSIA

Malaysia has a population of 21.6 million people, the smallest population among the Asian tigers. The core of the country lies on the Malay Peninsula. However, two other regions, Sabah and Sarawak, are located on the island of Borneo. Most Malaysians are Muslims of Malay origin, but there are also sizable Chinese and Indian minorities.

Since Singapore seceded from the country in the early 1960s, Malaysia has been extraordinarily successful in generating rapid growth. Initially, the country was a resource-based economy, exporting tin, palm oil, petroleum, and rubber, among other commodities. Subsequently, the country has developed major export industries in electronics, clothing, and shoes. These industries have helped generate very rapid rates of growth. Between 1993 and 1997, Malaysia reported growth rates averaging 8.6 percent per year, one of the most rapid growth rates among the tiger economies. However, some of this growth was financed by large current account deficits. In 1998, the current account deficit ran 5.1 percent of GDP.

Malaysia has been the only one of the tigers not to request a rescue program from the IMF. Initially, the government adopted a standard IMF response to pressures on its currency. Fiscal policy was tightened as government employees experienced reductions in real pay packets and as infrastructure investments were postponed. However, investors were treated to a series of policy disputes. Prime Minister Mahathir Mohamad accused "speculators" and Western governments of attacking the Malaysian currency. Former Deputy Prime Minister Anwar Ibrahim then followed with official statements, contradicting Mahathir's statements and attempting to sooth international investors. This state of affairs lasted through mid-1998, when Mahathir fired Anwar and placed him under arrest. At the same time, Mahathir reversed policy. Infrastructure investment has been revived, fiscal policy has been drastically loosened, and capital controls have been imposed, reducing the convertibility of the ringatt. GDP dropped sharply, falling 6.7 percent in 1998. GDP is forecast to contract by a modest 0.6 percent in 1999.

THE PHILIPPINES

The Philippines is an island nation of 75.1 million people. The country is in the middle of the other countries in Southeast Asia in terms of per capita income. At purchasing power parity rates, per capita income ran 2,600 1997 USD in 1998, substantially more than in the poorest nations of Burma and Cambodia but substantially less than in Malaysia or Singapore. At market exchange rates, GDP ran $70.8 billion in 1998.

Due to political instability, corruption, protectionism, and poor macroeconomic policies, the Philippines did not participate in the Southeast Asian boom in the 1980s. GDP growth was substantially lower than in other countries of the region, and in some years, the economy suffered recession. After the fall of Ferdinand Marcos, the democratic government of Corazon Aquino suffered from political instability that contributed to low growth rates. However, under Aquino and her successor, President Fidel Ramos, economic policy began to change. Trade was liberalized, state-owned companies were privatized, and fiscal and monetary policies were considerably tightened. In the 1990s, the country experienced a sharp acceleration in economic growth: GDP growth averaged 4.8 percent between 1994 and 1997. Furthermore, growth was more balanced than in the 1980s. Inflation averaged 7.7 percent per annum between 1993 and 1997. However, in some years the current account deficit ran close to 5 percent of GDP. Like other countries in Southeast Asia, the Philippines has experienced sharp declines in the value of its currency and in local stock markets since 1997. However, the country has not yet experienced the falls in output suffered by other countries in the region. The Philippines has benefited from a much stronger banking system than is present in the other countries, in part because foreign banks have been permitted to play a greater role domestically.

SINGAPORE

Like Hong Kong, Singapore is really a city-state. It serves as a financial and shipping center for Southeast Asia, especially for Malaysia and

Indonesia. Major industries include electronics, shipping, and finance. The country is predominantly Chinese but has sizable Indian and Malay minorities. Since leaving Malaysia shortly after independence in the early 1960s, Singapore has enjoyed one of the most rapid rates of economic growth ever reported by a country in modern history. Per capita GDP soared, hitting 27,865 1997 USD in purchasing power parity terms in 1998; at market exchange rates, per capita GDP was $26,308 in 1998, the highest rate in the region.

Per capita GDP has reached these high levels due to the rapid economic growth enjoyed by Singapore over the past three decades. In many years, GDP growth exceeded 9 percent. Between 1994 and 1997, GDP growth averaged 8.3 percent per year. Singapore has enjoyed very high savings rates, in part induced by government policy that compels citizens to save a substantial share of their income in retirement accounts. Investment levels have been very high. Despite this rapid growth in the past, Singapore has also been affected by the "Asian flu." Sharp declines in economic activity in Indonesia and Malaysia contributed to a decline in GDP in Singapore in 1998. However, the local currency has held up much better than those of its neighbors.

SOUTH KOREA

Technically, South Korea lies in Northeast, not Southeast, Asia but was included in the conference discussion because of the similarity of its rapid rates of growth since the early 1960s and its recent economic problems. South Korea has by far the largest economy among the countries discussed at the conference. At market exchange rates, GDP ran $442.5 billion in 1997. Per capita GDP was $6,585 at market exchange rates in 1998 and 14,560 1997 USD in purchasing power parity terms.

Like the other tigers, South Korea has enjoyed extraordinary rates of growth since 1960. In some periods, GDP rose over 9 percent per year. Between 1994 and 1997, GDP growth averaged 7.6 percent per year. Economic development in South Korea, however, has differed from the patterns seen in other countries. South Korea does not have the natural resource base of Indonesia or Malaysia, nor has it relied on foreign direct investment as has Singapore. The country's governments have chosen to restrict direct foreign investment and rely on borrowing to cover current account deficits. Governments have chosen local industrialists to lead economic growth. They have encouraged the development of highly leveraged conglomerates called *chaebols*. Unlike in Taiwan, where most economic output is produced by small- and medium-sized enterprises, in South Korea the large *chaebols* account for much of the country's GDP. Initially, many *chaebols* specialized in light industrial sectors, but early on the *chaebols* began to branch out into higher value-added sectors. Companies like Samsung, Daewoo, and Hyundai have moved into consumer electronics, shipbuilding, microchip manufacturing, and automobile assembly. The expansion of the *chaebols* was primarily funded by credit; these companies were extraordinarily leveraged by international standards. Their development was encouraged by the government through subsidized loans and directed credits. Since the Korean won began to fall in 1997 and interest rates began to rise, a number of the *chaebols* have come under severe financial pressure. Some have gone bankrupt, and others have had to severely retrench operations. The financial problems of the *chaebols* have been a major factor in the recession in South Korea. The economy contracted sharply in 1998, by 5.7 percent. South Korea's current account has moved into surplus, the won has stabilized, and interest rates are falling. Expanding exports and declining interest rates will be the key factors in a return to growth, but GDP is forecast to fall by 0.6 percent in 1999.

THAILAND

Thailand, with a population of 60.8 million people, is another of the miracle economies of Southeast Asia. Per capita GDP ran 6,700 1997 USD in 1998 at purchasing power parity rates. At market exchange rates, per capita GDP was much lower, only $1,953, in part because of the collapse of the local currency, the baht, in 1997. Since the 1960s, growth has been very rapid, spurred by solid increases in productivity in agriculture (Thailand is one of the largest exporters of rice in the world) and, more important, by a boom in light manufactures. More recently, Thailand has moved up-market as major multinationals have set up automobile and electronics assembly operations. Thailand's economy has also benefited from substantial revenues from tourism. As in the other countries, a construction boom, much of it financed by foreign borrowing, also boosted growth through 1997. Between 1994 and 1996, GDP growth averaged 8.1 percent per year, but in 1997 and 1998, GDP fell.

Thailand was the first country in the region to catch the "Asian flu." The rapid growth rates of the first half of 1990s were made possible by large current account deficits. A portion of the deficits was financed by direct foreign investment; Thailand was chosen as the location for a number of large, new plants at that time. However, a substantial part of this investment was financed by borrowing. Thai banks and finance companies borrowed dollars abroad and relent them to domestic borrowers, among them commercial real estate developers. With local short-term interest rates running 13 to 14 percent and an exchange rate pegged against the dollar, local banks made very attractive spreads by borrowing in dollars and lending in baht. However, by 1996, the current account deficit hit 8 percent of GDP, another in several years of large deficits. Foreign lenders began to cut credit to Thailand, and local banks and other institutions began to purchase dollars to reduce exchange-rate risk. Eventually, the central bank was unable to support the currency and had to let the currency float; the baht fell 35 percent. Much of the banking system was found to be insolvent. Thailand became the first recipient of an IMF program and also began to clean up its banking system aggressively. Like South Korea, Thailand has already moved into current account surplus. The rapid sale of assets and bankrupt enterprises has encouraged a number of foreign investors to purchase banks and companies in the country. The inflow of foreign capital has helped stabilize the currency and restart export operations and contributed to a decline in real interest rates. Although unemployment is likely to continue to rise, recovery may be in sight for Thailand in 2000. GDP is forecast to fall by 2.3 percent in 1999.

The "Washington Consensus" and the Crisis in Southeast Asia

In contrast to Southeast Europe, where most countries reported declining output for a number of years, Southeast Asia experienced a period of strong growth in the early 1990s. By 1997 a number of these countries, most notably Indonesia, Malaysia, Singapore, and Thailand, had enjoyed over two decades of very strong growth, averaging over 8 percent per year. These growth rates were among the highest ever reported in the world. This phenomenal growth was attributed to high rates of saving, relatively open trading regimes, rising levels of education, fairly low rates of inflation, and stable exchange rates. Because of the success of these states, in the early 1990s countries such as the Philippines and Vietnam, which had lagged their neighbors in terms of economic growth, adopted some of the economic policies of their neighbors in hopes of mimicking the success. Both the Philippines and Vietnam succeeded in raising growth rates.

A number of commentators have ascribed these rapid rates of growth to economic policies advocated first by the Reagan and Thatcher administrations and by subsequent U.S. and British governments. This set of policies, known as the "Washington Consensus," consists of tight monetary and fiscal policies, free trade, and liberalized capital flows.

In 1997, these countries ran into severe economic difficulties. A number of countries had run large current account deficits, substantial portions of which were financed by short-term borrowing from abroad or by sales of local currency bonds to foreign investors. Because of fixed exchange rates, many local companies found it more attractive to borrow in dollars than in local currencies. During the early years of rapid economic growth, rates of return on invested capital tended to be relatively high. However, the large influx of capital in the 1990s was not always put to such good use. Much of it was used to finance factories, commercial real estate, and even golf courses that have not been able to generate expected rates of return. Consequently, loans have not been repaid, and many banks have become insolvent. The resulting sharp contraction in credit has precipitated very deep recessions in Indonesia, South Korea, and Thailand.

According to the IMF, policy weaknesses are the underlying reason for the Southeast Asian economic problems.[2] Inflexible exchange-rate regimes were maintained too long, constraining the response of monetary policy to increasing macroeconomic disequilibrium. Investors took the pegged-exchange-rate regimes as government guarantees and acted accordingly. In addition, banking supervision was lax. Implicit government guarantees on loans, combined with corruption and rapid growth in international funds available to invest in emerging markets, resulted in an accumulation of bad loans and the erosion of balance sheets in the banking system. Because of these structural problems, when foreign investors changed their perceptions and began to withdraw capital from the domestic economies, the adjustment was much more severe than would have been the case if economic policy had addressed these problems in the banking sector more quickly.

A number of these countries have turned to the IMF for support during this period of turmoil. The IMF has arranged major programs of financial assistance for three of the countries: Indonesia, South Korea, and Thailand. The basic principles underlying these programs are consistent with the "Washington Consensus" described above. The policy mix generally advocated by the IMF for these countries can be summarized as follows:

1. The IMF encouraged the governments to tighten fiscal policy to reassure foreign investors and to assist in shifting resources to net exports in order to reduce the current account deficits.
2. Monetary policies had to be kept sufficiently tight to mitigate against excessive declines in exchange rates. However, once confidence was restored, the IMF supported a gradual reduction in rates so as not to choke off recovery.
3. The financial systems needed to be recapitalized and restructured. Confidence in the systems had to be restored immediately,

and bankrupt institutions had to be liquidated. Bank supervision still needs to be dramatically improved.

4. Economic and financial data needed to be improved and dispensed on a timelier basis and more broadly.

A number of commentators have criticized the appropriateness of the "Washington Consensus" as policies for rapid growth. Critics of the "Washington Consensus" argue that this set of policy prescriptions results in premature liberalization of capital markets and too little attention to the solvency of the banking sector. In particular, they argue that capital markets frequently "overshoot": they provide too much capital for the available investment opportunities when times appear to be good, stimulating investment in highly risky and unprofitable projects; when times are bad, capital markets overreact and withdraw capital from solvent, profitable businesses. The resulting decline in the availability of credit has led to the current deep recessions.

Commentators have also taken issue with the policy mix advocated by the IMF to stabilize these economies. Some commentators have argued that fiscal tightening was unnecessary because budgets were already in surplus. Some have argued that the emphasis on closing insolvent banks contributed to the sharp decline in credit and thereby worsened the current recessions and made adjustment more difficult as exporters have been unable to obtain loans to expand operations. Others have criticized the program for not imposing greater costs on investors. They have accused the IMF of bailing out unwise investment decisions. These critics argue that in the future, investors will assume that the IMF will again provide resources to forestall default. Acting on these assumptions, investors will continue to make the same mistakes, contributing to a series of future crises.

The resolution of these disputes will have to await the resumption of growth in Southeast Europe and Southeast Asia. However, the conference proceedings summarized below provide a number of insights on these issues and are directed toward illuminating current disputes and creating a consensus on the policy responses most effective for contributing to a resumption of sustainable growth in both regions.

Notes

[1] We would like to thank Standard & Poor's *DRI* for graciously providing much of the information for this section. It draws heavily on Standard & Poor's *DRI's World Economic Outlook*.

[2] This discussion is based on "The Asian Crisis," chapter 5 of the *Annual Report of the International Monetary Fund*, 1998.

Chapter 3

The Rise and Fall of Emerging Markets

Clearly, the Asian currency and financial crisis has had, and will continue to have, enormous international consequences. For the first half of 1998, there was hope that Asia's problems could be dealt with and that the region's economic difficulties would not spill over to other parts of the world. The events of late August and early September showed how vain those hopes were. Not only has the turmoil in Asia proven to be a prelude to currency and financial crises in Russia and Latin America, but Asia's problems have also severely tested the IMF. The IMF's difficulties in coping with the crisis in Asia, and now in other regions, raise serious questions about the ability of the international community to manage economic crises. The turmoil in Asia, Russia, and now Latin America also raises fundamental questions about how, in an increasingly global economy, the developed world should assist emerging markets. These troubling developments form the backdrop for the governments of other countries—such as those in Southeast Europe—committed to continued economic transition. The two opening addresses of the conference provided a picture of the evolution of the crisis in Southeast Asia and an examination of the current situation in Southeast Europe.

Southeast Asia

In many ways, the four countries hit hardest by the Asian currency and financial crisis in 1997–98 seemed unlikely candidates for trouble. Over the last three decades, Malaysia, Indonesia, Thailand, and South Korea have done much that was right in macroeconomic terms. Indeed, the beginning of the currency crisis in July 1997 came as a surprise to most of the leadership in Southeast Asia, as well as to foreign investors in these countries.

Participants in this session discussed both the origins of the crisis in Southeast Asia and the consequent challenges to the "Washington Consensus." Some discussants suggested that the dilemma for the international community is how to maximize the benefits of free-flowing international capital while minimizing its negative impact. What went wrong in Southeast Asia, according to some of the participants, is that the structures of free-market institutions in emerging markets were not developed fully enough to face the rigors of the international capital and currency markets. Therefore, the international community should more clearly recognize that the creation of market regimes and institutions needs to be more advanced before emerging markets are subjected to the rigors of global capital and currency markets.

ORIGINS OF A CRISIS

Before discussing what went wrong, and why, we need to remember what was achieved in Southeast Asia and how the countries in the region made the progress they did. Their progress was the source of much of the confidence that fueled the optimism about future prospects in Southeast Asia and in emerging markets in other parts of the world. In recent decades, Indonesia, South Korea, Malaysia, and Thailand enjoyed extraordinary rates of growth. In each of these countries in the 1990s, GDP per capita grew at an annual rate of at least 5 percent. This accomplishment was based on solid achievements in other areas. All four countries have high rates of savings, each saving around one-third of GDP. These countries also had general government surpluses in 1996–97. Surpluses ran 1.6 percent of GDP in Thailand and 1.4 percent in Indonesia. Inflation in each of the countries was also low.

The gains these countries made positively affected the lives of ordinary citizens as poverty was sharply reduced. In 1975, 60 percent of Southeast Asians lived on less than $1 a day; in 1996, the percentage was 20 percent. Indonesia, perhaps the hardest hit by the crisis, had achieved much in the previous decades. Between 1975 and 1995, the poverty rate in Indonesia had declined from 64 percent to 11 percent of the population.

Development policies became unbalanced in the 1990s as governments attempted to maintain high growth rates, stable rates of exchange, increasing flows of foreign investment, and government guarantees to participants in poorly regulated financial markets. The result was a boom in real estate and securities markets, overvalued currencies, and increasing current account deficits. The last were financed by banks taking out short-term, hard-currency loans on the assumption that exchange rates would be stable and that governments would back up the banks if they got into difficulty. In the spring of 1997, financial markets began to limit further access to credit as they questioned both the ability of countries to maintain sizable trade deficits and the worsening foreign debt-to-GDP ratios.

The very large current account deficits and reliance on foreign capital to finance these deficits, coupled with poorly functioning domestic banking systems and the failure of government policymakers to quickly adjust exchange rates and other policy instruments to an environment of reduced availability of capital, produced the 1997 currency and financial crisis. There is also a strong consensus among most observers that the extended period of economic stagnation in Japan played an important part in the Southeast Asian crisis. Japan's sluggish economy in the 1990s led to a slowdown in the growth of Southeast Asian commodity and manufactured exports to Japan. Exacerbating the situation was the weakening position of the yen. Since some of the Southeast Asian countries' currencies were pegged to the dollar, they became less competitive in Asian markets as the dollar appieciated against the yen.

Japan's problems also played a role in encouraging the Southeast Asian accumulation of short-term commercial debt denominated in foreign currencies. Because of the low interest rates in Japan—the result of government policy to stimulate domestic investment—its banks sought greater returns elsewhere, including the countries of Southeast Asia, where Japanese banks invested heavily in yen-denominated short-term loans. They were of course not alone. Favorable interest rates also attracted European and U.S. banks to what appeared to be a lucrative business of making short-term loans to Southeast Asian banks and companies in strong Western currencies. In the face of depreciating local currencies, these obligations became more expensive for local borrowers to repay. These troubled loans precipitated the economic collapse of banks and enterprises in Thailand, South Korea, and Indonesia and triggered sharp declines in output and massive outflows of capital.

HOW THE CRISIS SPREAD

On the most elemental level, the Asian crisis undermined the confidence of financial markets. To sustain the mid-1990s high level of capital flows into emerging markets, investors needed a high degree of confidence that the economies in Asia, and elsewhere, would continue to grow. Thailand's currency crisis in July 1997 caused second thoughts about other countries in the region. Within months of the first signs of turmoil in Thailand, dampened investor enthusiasm caused problems in Malaysia, Indonesia, the Philippines, and South Korea.

By the middle of 1998, the crisis had spread outside of the region. Investors came to believe that if a currency and financial crisis could hobble Southeast Asia, then it could happen anywhere. Thus, events in Asia heightened the nervousness of financial markets about other emerging markets. Also undermining confidence was Japan's continued inability, even after the election of a new government, to cope with the country's profound economic problems. Events in the United States did not help: the anticipation of the end of the stock market boom also undermined the general confidence of financial markets in the near-term future of both developed and emerging markets.

Within a little over a year of the first signs of trouble in Thailand, the contagion spread to Russia and Latin America. To be sure, Russia's long-term problems had been a concern of financial markets for some time. The weakness of the country's banking system, coupled with the inability of its government to collect taxes and to follow a coherent set of economic reforms, contributed to undermine the confidence of financial markets. Foreign capital began to flow out a few months after the Asian crisis gathered steam, soon accompanied by the capital of domestic investors looking for more secure places to invest. The Russian collapse has already affected economies closely tied to Russia, particularly Ukraine and Belarus, and could hurt Central and Southeast Europe. Sharp drops in oil and gas prices, reducing Russia's foreign-currency earnings and tax revenues, exacerbated the country's internal economic problems. The crisis in Russia resulted in significant losses for Western investors. Some investors had borrowed money to invest in Russia. As the value of their Russian assets sagged, their creditors called in collateral for these margin loans. These calls forced investors in Russian securities to liquidate their holdings. In some instances, the value of their Russian assets had fallen so sharply that these investors were forced to liquidate assets in other markets as well.

Investors' need for cash has contributed, at least initially, to the turmoil in Latin American equity and currency markets. Falling commodity prices also affected the financial markets' confidence in Latin American countries. Mexico and Venezuela have been receiving lower oil prices; Chile and Peru have faced declining copper prices; and Argentina is now getting lower prices for agricultural products. Latin American governments are trying to stem the capital outflow by raising interest rates. Whether they succeed remains to be seen. What is certain is that high interest rates will slow the economies of countries forced to adopt them.

IMPLICATIONS FOR THE INTERNATIONAL COMMUNITY

In considering the broader international implications of the Asian crisis, we see that it is not only financial markets that have suffered an erosion of confidence. The events of the last fourteen months have implicitly challenged the faith put in the "Washington Consensus" that emerged during the Thatcher and Reagan years. Deregulation, privatization, trade liberalization, and free-flowing capital have continued to be the central precepts of British and U.S. policy toward the international economic system since that time. The increasing attention to slowing volatile capital flows by regulating them in some way is an important challenge to the received wisdom of the last decade and a half. In addition, the crisis has invited harsh criticism of the apparent inability of the IMF, one of the pillars of the international economic order put in place after World War II, to cope with the crisis.

Total private capital flows to emerging markets increased five and a half times between 1990 ($44.4 billion) and 1996 ($243.8 billion). In 1990, 55 percent of these flows represented foreign direct investment (FDI), that is, investments made by companies in subsidiaries abroad; only 12 percent was portfolio investment, that is, easily liquidated investments in stocks and bonds; commercial loans, that is, loans made by foreign banks to emerging market borrowers, accounted for 7 percent. In 1996, FDI was 45 percent; portfolio investment grew to 38 percent; and commercial loans were 14 percent of total capital flows to emerging markets. Consequently, when portfolio investors began to withdraw funds in 1997 and 1998, they had a very appreciable impact on total capital flows.

Some economists have begun to question whether countries open to volatile capital flows really benefit in terms of higher rates of growth. India and China restrict inflows of both FDI and portfolio capital, and they have recently registered high growth rates while largely avoiding the turmoil found elsewhere in Asia. Beginning in the early 1980s, Chile limited frenetic capital movements and seems to have been less affected by the current difficulties in Latin America as are other countries in the region. It remains to be seen what will happen to Malaysia now that its prime minister has decided to take steps to drastically limit the convertibility of the currency, in effect cutting Malaysia off from global financial markets.

The dilemma for the international community is how to maximize the benefits of capital availability while minimizing the negative impact of capital careening around international markets. Clearly, there should be ways to encourage longer-term debt and more FDI, which, by definition, is committed for a longer period and often brings with it technology and managerial skills.

As troubling as the Southeast Asian crisis has been to individual countries in the region, it has also pointed to disturbing questions about the adequacy of the major institutions of the international economic system to manage the crisis. The focus of criticism has been on the IMF. Critics have blasted the IMF for its failure to anticipate the crisis in Asia and then, when confronted with the turmoil, for its failure to apply appropriate remedies.

The debates over capital flows and the IMF suggest the need for a review of the international economy's approach to emerging markets.

It is theoretically correct that there are benefits to deregulation, privatization, and freer markets. What seems to have been wrong in Southeast Asia is that the structures of free-market institutions in emerging markets were not developed fully enough to face the rigors of the international capital and currency markets. Clearly, the Asian crisis illustrates that in emerging markets, the capabilities of governments and private financial and business institutions are as important as the discipline of the market. Effective markets do not just happen. They require systems of commercial law, clear accounting standards, and professional public administration. Together, these systems create the rules for, and the smooth operations of, the public and private institutions central to market activity.

The issue is not the simpleminded proposition of "more versus less government intervention in the economy." It is a matter of the "right versus the wrong" kind of government intervention. In the Southeast Asian countries, governments have frequently interfered in credit allocation, directing banks to favored lenders. This "crony capitalism" has been very expensive as many of the financed projects have failed. The need to build market structures in developing countries is not news to the IMF, the World Bank, and other major actors in the international economy. The World Bank has supported many of the structural elements necessary for market development for over a decade. Since the 1994–95 crisis in Mexico, the IMF has been studying how to better avoid crises and how to better deal with them when they inevitably do occur. Obviously, more needs to be done.

Southeast Europe

As the countries in Southeast Europe prepare for eventual membership in the European Union (EU) and other international financial organizations, each country is beginning from a different point. Slovenia is on one end of the spectrum, preparing for EU membership early in the next century, while Albania is the only remaining developing country in Europe. The countries in Southeast Europe are also integrated with world organizations at different levels. In addition to Slovenia, Bulgaria and Romania have signed Association Agreements with the EU. Macedonia, Bosnia-Herzegovina, and Croatia have less-comprehensive agreements. Yugoslavia remains much more isolated. The countries' relationships with Europe may have helped shield them from the negative consequences of the crisis in Southeast Asia. The different ways in which each country finances its transformation alter the character of the transition in that country. Association or Europe Agreements with the EU entitle a country to increased levels of foreign aid from the EU, usually through the EU's PHARE assistance program.

THE STATUS OF THE TRANSITIONS

In Southeast Europe, the transformation has not happened in a calm or balanced political atmosphere. The potential for ethnic conflict in several countries in the region is a barrier to transition. The former Yugoslav republics continue to suffer from hangover effects from the war in Bosnia, although Slovenia is now fairly insulated from further violence. In Romania and Bulgaria, homegrown economic crises were brought about by an attempt to hang on to the old system rather than reforming.

As these countries restructure their economies, their markets must also be reoriented. During the socialist era, the main market for Southeast European goods was the Soviet Union. Although the Russian market remains very attractive for agricultural goods, the markets now need to be oriented to the West. However, an almost irrational attachment to EU markets as the single Western-bound orientation has developed. This reliance on the EU caused problems in 1995 and 1996 when demand from the EU was weaker than expected and when substantial direct foreign investment from the EU failed to materialize. Investment from the EU has been low in part because of continued political instability in the region.

In most of these countries, the major homework of economic restructuring has been done. Prices have been liberalized. Markets and foreign trade have been liberalized and opened to competition. A legislative framework, including new laws for bankruptcy, has been put into place. Many of the banks have been restructured.

However, privatization remains a stumbling block in many countries, contributing to the continued weakness of institutions. Both Bulgaria and Romania have yet to complete the privatization of agricultural land and housing; both still have not completely resolved which properties are to be restored to presocialist owners. In both countries, many farmers have yet to obtain formal title to their newly acquired land. Romania continues to run large budget deficits. The last chance for true institutional reform in Yugoslavia passed with the dismissal of Central Bank Governor Avramovic. Privatization is also quite slow in Croatia. Wide-ranging privatization efforts during the past two years in Macedonia have greatly improved conditions there. Two-thirds of Macedonian GDP is now in private hands.

Fiscal and monetary policies vary greatly throughout the region. The regimes followed in Slovenia, Croatia, and Macedonia have been quite successful in reducing inflation. Romanian policies are improved, but struggles with the budget continue, and the stabilization policies recently led to the dismissal of the finance minister because the policies were politically unpopular. In Bulgaria, budget discipline has been restored under the Kostov government, and inflation has been scaled down. Albanian fiscal and monetary policies have recently been questionable. In Yugoslavia, policy has been jeopardized by politics after the central bank governor tried to radically restructure fiscal and monetary policy. Economic policy in Yugoslavia differs from republic to republic. Serbia and Montenegro have undertaken separate privatization programs. Montenegro has sent out signals that it will try to press on with radical reforms. The EU has attempted to encourage market reforms in Montenegro by providing more open-market access to exports from Montenegro, if the republic can demonstrate that the exports are produced entirely in Montenegro.

The banking sector throughout the region requires continued restructuring and development. Many banks remain undercapitalized. In large measure, the banking sector remains under state control. Capital markets are limited by the lack of progress in privatization. Stock exchanges have only recently been opened in these countries, and turnover remains very limited.

RELATIONS WITH THE INTERNATIONAL COMMUNITY

Among the EU-associated countries, Slovenia is already well integrated with the EU. Bulgaria and Romania each receive a significant amount of support, but investors remain hesitant to enter either country. EU membership will not be possible for ten to fifteen years.

The postwar countries are under a special EU program. They have not signed Europe Agreements but are subject to agreements with a high decree of conditionality. Bosnia-Herzegovina will require aid for many years. Aid has thus far been massive. Foreign investment has begun to drip in, including the start of automobile assembly by Volkswagen's Czech subsidiary Skoda in Sarajevo. Recovery of industrial output in Bosnia-Herzegovina is not guaranteed to continue, but 15 to 20 percent growth is expected in 1998, from a very low base. The EU has intimated that Croatian exporters will be given preferential access to EU markets only if the Croatian government improves human rights policies, especially regarding the treatment of Serbian refugees. Rapid growth will continue, but Croatia continues to face problems with balance of payments.

Other countries include Albania and Macedonia. Albania is a subsistence economy in which substantial amounts of consumer goods are purchased in open-air markets. Albanians go abroad to purchase these goods, or Albanian workers abroad ship these goods home; this "shuttle trade" provides a very substantial share of retail sales in Albania. Macedonia enjoyed a slow recovery of 2.4 percent in 1997 after a successful transformation; growth may reach 4 percent in 1998. Although these economies have unsophisticated banking systems, they are also less vulnerable to outside crises. A low level of financial intermediation is typically viewed as a minus, but currently it may be a plus.

IMPACT OF THE CRISIS IN SOUTHEAST ASIA

The key indicators point toward continued instability. The economic data on Southeast Asia are currently much more negative than those on Southeast Europe. The World Bank sees Southeast Europe, as a region, as less indebted. However, current account deficits remain higher than expected, and they cannot be maintained in the long term.

Although the crisis in Southeast Asia triggered a general loss of confidence in emerging markets, foreign-exchange markets remained calm in Southeast Europe. Stock markets did fall, but they also fell in the West. Southeast Europe has faced higher debt-servicing costs as interest rates have risen, and official reserves have been used to defend local currencies.

The Russian crisis has had a greater impact on Southeast Europe. Because the smaller countries have limited access to private international capital markets, the financial fallout from Russia was limited for them. However, Romania has faced difficulties rolling over its debts, and the risk that international banks associate with lending to Croatia has risen. More important, some of the countries have experienced sharp declines in exports to Russia and the other former Soviet republics. Bulgaria, in particular, has been hard hit.

Overall, the economies of Southeast Europe were not damaged by the "Asian flu" as severely as might have been expected, although the Russian crisis is hurting some countries. In part, this may be a result of the closer ties between the Southeast European economies and the EU. Following the introduction of the euro, the block of EU countries, dubbed Euroland, will be able to more effectively resist global crises as this new reserve currency replaces a multitude of weaker currencies. A majority is now convinced that the euro will be successful, since confidence in the single European currency is growing, especially in the business sector. The close ties of the Southeast European countries to the EU and currency links to the new euro are likely to cushion Southeast Europe from the full brunt of the Asian and Russian crises.

Chapter 4

The IMF and Economic Sovereignty: Institutional Responses

This conference session focused on the constraints on central banks in managing economies in crisis or in transition. In particular, the benefits and restrictions of currency boards and other exchange-rate regimes were examined in detail. The session also dealt, explicitly and implicitly, with conditionality. The IMF and governments that turn to it for support negotiate various programs under which the governments promise to implement specified policy measures and the IMF provides financial support. The loans become conditional on the implementation of the promised policies. In the case of Southeast Asia, the agreements with the IMF have included both promises to change monetary, fiscal, and exchange-rate policies and promises to create or reform institutions. This session investigated the successes and failures of imposing conditions as part of macroeconomic stabilization programs and the institutional prerequisites to make such programs work.

Conditionality has two facets: the visible hand and the invisible hand. The visible hand includes the specified policy measures to which the governments and the IMF agree and the institutions through which these measures are implemented. The invisible hand includes the set of constraints imposed by the international economic and financial environment. International financial markets impose implicit conditionality on countries by denying capital to those countries that fail to adopt economic policies in which investors have trust. Market forces are often less transparent but are a more effective way to impose macroeconomic discipline than conditions explicitly imposed by international financial institutions. Historically, market conditionality has been the dominant constraint on small, open economies.

Central Banks, Currency Boards, and Conditionality

This session examined the implementation of a currency board in Bulgaria and discussed some of the lessons that can be learned from Bulgaria's experience. In particular, it examined how the roles of governments and central banks are changed under a currency board regime. The session also investigated how Indonesia fell victim to the "Asian flu" and why it was forced to look to the IMF for help. The session examined why a currency board was not an acceptable solution given Indonesia's circumstances, even though the idea was floated. Indonesia's recent difficulties can provide lessons on how financial liberalization should proceed.

BULGARIA

In Bulgaria, the invisible hand of conditionality has long been present. Bondholders in the first part of the century were extremely powerful. Following World War I, the monetary policy regime in force was very similar to a currency board. Among other things, the Inter-Allied Commission held a veto power on decisions of the central bank. A similar arrangement existed under the Financial Committee of the League of Nations during the 1930s.

In July 1997, a currency board was introduced in Bulgaria. Currency in circulation is now required to be equal to official reserves of foreign exchange plus monetary gold converted into leva at a specified rate to the deutsche mark. The Issue Department of the Bulgarian National Bank is required to exchange leva for deutsche marks at a rate of BGL 1,000 to the deutsche mark or at a rate within a band of 0.5 percent of the fixed ratio.

The ultimate goals of the currency board are quite simple. A currency board is implemented to eliminate the main causes of monetary indiscipline, the deepest cause of which is always fiscal indiscipline. Adherence to the currency board assists in the creation of credible institutions. It also helps to remonetize the economy and to rebuild the financial system after money has practically disappeared. Finally, a currency board helps to open the economy and to achieve full convertibility.

A currency board clearly imposes more constraints on policymakers than do more traditional arrangements such as pegged- or floating-rate systems. Typically, a currency board is imposed when a country is slow to reform structurally. In Bulgaria, the currency board arrangement was imposed by consensus following the experience of the first years of the transition. It was conceived as a tool for imposing financial discipline rather than as a simple stabilization scheme. The currency board was designed to overcome the deeply rooted reluctance to modernize the Bulgarian economy after seven years of piecemeal, inconsistent, and incomprehensible "reforms." It was also a means to deal with the institutional failures of the first years of the transition.

Parallels can be seen between the institution of a currency board and the former adherence to the gold standard. Historically, the gold standard was the best-known mechanism to impose strong macroeconomic discipline on a country from outside. In a sense, the currency board is a return to the goals and automatism of the gold standard.

A currency board is more vulnerable to international shocks than are "classic" monetary instruments. It shifts the burden of adjustment from changes in the exchange rate or other financial instruments directly to the economic actors in a country, that is, consumers and enterprises. It also disciplines policymakers by forcing them to adjust fiscal policy to the constraints imposed by the board. The burden of adjustment falls on the "real" sector—consumption and production—rather than on financial flows. Currency boards also make countries heavily dependent on inflows of capital. The more prone to external shocks an economy is and the less able to respond to them, the more subject it is to market conditionality. Despite the fixed exchange rate, a currency board arrangement is not a completely rigid arrangement. Reserves act as one shock absorber, and the system has only one fixed price—the exchange rate.

On the surface, the main institutional loser following the introduction of a currency board appears to be the central bank. After the establishment of the currency board, the central bank no longer regulates the money supply; after a board is established, markets and the exogenous decisions of economic agents autonomously determine the money supply. The money supply is anchored by fixing the exchange rate. Monetary sovereignty has been transferred abroad as the money supply depends on capital inflows. The central bank has also lost its control over the monetary base because the domestic components of money creation, normally managed by a central bank, have disappeared. Short-term liquidity management is abandoned because the central bank no longer has control over fluctuations in interest rates and no longer intervenes in foreign-exchange markets. In addition, the central bank may no longer refinance the banking system or government or act as the lender of last resort.

In theory, the Bulgarian central bank had been awarded a great deal of autonomy under the previous regime, but it was not able to exercise an autonomous policy in practice. Instead, the central bank was strongly limited by the government. Within the framework of the floating-exchange-rate regime, the central bank was unable to control inflation or the exchange rate when holders of leva lost confidence in the currency. Even after interest rates were raised to nearly prohibitive levels in 1996, the currency still failed to respond.

In practice, the implementation of a currency board produced important shifts in the balance of economic power and, consequently, in the financial flows of the economy. The central bank lost some powers but gained others. It is now under firm budgetary constraints and no longer has "hidden" resources gained by inflationary financing. Under a pegged exchange rate, the central bank must simultaneously manage domestic liquidity and the capital account, inevitably resulting in policies that invite a speculative attack. However, institutional changes provide the bank with more power to regulate and supervise the banking sector. In addition, the bank was made more independent from governmental control because any direct financing of fiscal deficits was eliminated.

As a small, open economy, Bulgaria is highly constrained in its ability to pursue economic policies that generate large budget or current account deficits because its access to international financial markets has been quite limited. The government is also constrained by external geostrategic influences. Instituting a currency board arrangement limits the strategic choices for the economy, but usually in an environment in which the country has very limited policy-making ability in any event. Institutional lending has often been accompanied by strong conditions, since creditors have long had the implicit right to impose conditions.

By restructuring capital flows and Bulgaria's debt burden, the implementation of a currency board has had an important impact on the place of the government in the economy. The economic position of the government has been changed because expenditures can no longer rise across the board. However, as a result of tighter fiscal policies and debt restructuring, the constraints imposed by Bulgaria's debt burden have been significantly relaxed, and the government must now figure out what to do with the money no longer needed for debt servicing. Previously, the burden of internal debt had limited the government's role in making effective policy choices.

Commercial bank behavior has also been altered following the inflationary period from 1996 to 1997 and the creation of the currency board. The lack of effective supervision and the continuous "socialization" of state and private bank losses through the budget and the central bank from 1991 to 1996 led to a deep financial crisis and the eventual closing of fourteen commercial banks. After July 1997, the banks adopted a very cautious attitude and credit policies based on a strong aversion to risk. The outcome has been a generalized credit restraint that approaches a credit crunch, as well as a dramatic improvement in the liquidity position of the commercial banks. Now banks need to decide where to invest their liquidity, but the choices remain limited: loans (but low risk), government bonds or bills (but there is now less government debt to finance), or deposits in foreign banks abroad.

From 1991 to 1996, the trend in Bulgaria was for the real sector to adjust to different types of shocks through arrears, bad debts, and the devaluation of the lev. These monetary instruments are no longer available under a currency board arrangement. Under the new regime, the economy must adjust through real variables such as productivity and output as well as through greater financial discipline. However, the change of mentality required in the real sector appears to be the most difficult aspect of the transition, even with the strong constraints of the currency board in place. The currency board provides the economic agents with a framework of financial stability, long-term outlook, and broader choice. However, the benefits of the new economic environment can be realized only by sizable investment in the economy.

The private and public sectors both need to restructure in order to better face the inevitable real effective appreciation of the currency that will occur as a result of the currency board. Before the introduction of the currency board, the household sector had been totally removed from financial channels. Currently, it is being reincorporated into the financial sector. The restructuring of capital flows in the economy has permitted households access to some credit resources. An increase in lending to households, mainly through the State Savings Bank, has expanded consumer credit.

The first year of the currency board has generally been considered a success in both Bulgaria and abroad. Success was due to the careful design and preparation of the board. Ironically, in the case of Bulgaria, the disappearance of money in the economy due to the demonetization caused by hyperinflation greatly facilitated the introduction of the currency board. At the beginning of 1997, the Bulgarian economy was almost completely dollarized; there was a high potential for default on foreign debt and for a de facto default on domestic debt through hyperinflation triggered by a continuous monetization of fiscal deficits. Implementation of a currency board was the only appropriate arrangement to restore confidence in the national currency and in the financial system as a whole. However, implementation of the currency board was also facilitated by a change in regime. The former governments had been discredited because of the failure of their economic policies. The new regime, untainted by the failures of past policies, had much more credibility.

The currency board has raised the international standing of Bulgaria. Bulgaria has benefited from its newly acquired international recognition as a trendsetter in the world economy. A number of governments and banks have spoken highly of Bulgaria's decision; because of the stability provided by the currency board, investors have begun to put money into the Bulgarian economy. The Bulgarian government is proud of the IMF's recognition of the success of this policy; the IMF only rarely supports the introduction of a currency board. Policymakers are examining the Bulgarian currency board as a possible model for countries facing deep economic troubles, like Russia and Indonesia.

The IMF has taken an active role in Bulgaria as part of an attempt by the organization to regain credibility. The IMF had been losing respect because the previous, failed economic policies instituted in Bulgaria were accompanied by IMF standby agreements under which the IMF provided loans in support of Bulgaria's balance of payments and the Bulgarian government committed itself to make changes in its economic policies. Through these agreements, the IMF played a central role in the legitimization of economic policy. Explicitly or implicitly, it provided some "imported" credibility to the policies of the Bulgarian government and shifted some of the responsibility for these policies abroad. Since the IMF shared some responsibility with the government, it lost credibility, along with the government, when stabilization programs repeatedly failed.

Looking back on the experience of Bulgaria, we can gather some clear lessons regarding the timing for the introduction of a currency board:

1. The right time for introduction of a currency board is after hyperinflation. Currency boards are most easily introduced following the demolition of the economy.
2. Currency boards are best introduced following clear political change. A currency board is not viable under an unchanged and compromised political regime.
3. Because emissions of local currency are tied to reserves of foreign currency, currency boards are implicitly financed from abroad. In Bulgaria's case, the financing came from the IMF.
4. The only important domestic choice is the selection of the reserve currency. Bulgaria chose the deutsche mark, although much of its foreign debt is denominated in dollars and much of the economy is dollarized. However, the strategic link to the deutsche mark and the shift to the euro are important political and economic choices in light of Bulgaria's desire to eventually join the EU.

The early results of the Bulgarian currency board can be summarized into two general categories. The first group consisted of largely expected outcomes:

1. Disinflation occurred even faster than expected. The main channel of inflation—fiscal policy—has been removed, but other sources linked to the structural and market deficiencies in the economy remain. However, since the beginning of 1998, the inflation rate has been close to zero.

2. Interest rates have fallen dramatically. They have not quite declined to German rates, but central rates are around 5 to 6 percent and other rates are 12 to 15 percent.
3. There has been a net inflow of foreign resources. During 1998, Bulgaria achieved a sizable surplus on the current and capital accounts. Foreign investment remains an important source of external financing.
4. The credibility of the financial system is improving, but a longer period of stability is needed to overcome the shock of the previous financial collapse.

The second category included more ambiguous results:

1. Although Bulgarians are beginning to replace dollars with leva in local transactions and bank lending and although other forms of financial intermediation are expanding, the pace at which the economy is being "remonetized" is relatively slow. After a strong increase in the second half of 1997, broad money and other monetary aggregates were flat in 1998.
2. The banking sector is financially sound but passive.
3. The real sector is reviving from a very low starting point, but this is not the type of revival expected. In comparison with Estonia and Argentina, which also have currency boards, Bulgaria has experienced a later revival of the real sector. Some loopholes for hidden subsidies and soft budget constraints are still in place, although most of them are to be eliminated in the framework of the three-year extended arrangement with the IMF.
4. The government is under harder budget constraints concerning domestic revenues and expenditures. A considerable effort in the first half of 1998 resulted in a buildup of an important fiscal reserve account. External debt service, however, will require the infusion of foreign financing through the medium term.

The Bulgarian currency board has not yet been tested by a major exogenous shock. The world financial crisis has not had a direct impact on Bulgaria due to the underdeveloped financial systems in Bulgaria. Along with the stability provided by the currency board, the limited amount of direct foreign investment and portfolio investment has also helped to shield Bulgaria.

However, a downside risk does exist for Bulgaria if the Southeast Asian crisis continues to become more globalized. Bulgaria could be hit directly (or indirectly) by a depression in world prices of major Bulgarian exports such as bulk chemicals, ferrous metals, and refined oil products. The economy could also be hit by the contagion of further declines in world stock markets. There may also be significant consequences for Bulgaria stemming specifically from the crisis in Russia. Substantial shares of Bulgarian exports go to Russia and other former Soviet republics. The resulting decline in demand for these products could slow economic growth. Lastly, Bulgaria still requires a great deal of foreign investment, and international investors may be frightened away by continued turbulence in emerging markets.

No time limit has been set for the currency board, and no changes in the monetary system are planned in the foreseeable future. Clearly, the currency board must last long enough to be effective. In the context of future accession to the EU, the natural transition from a currency board is to join the European Monetary Union. As a result, Bulgaria views the currency board as an important step toward EU membership, since the operation of a currency board is very similar to working under "EMU-like" conditions. Although Bulgaria is unlikely to enter the EU with the currency board still in place, the experience assists the Bulgarian central bank to act like other European central banks. The currency board also helps to stabilize the macroeconomic parameters of the economy over the long term and paves the way for convergence toward the Maastricht criteria.

INDONESIA

In Indonesia, the question of what is left for a sovereign country to do in the midst of an international rescue agreement is quite acute. Since the 1970s, Indonesia has worked to liberalize its capital account. With the rupiah freely convertible since that time, there have been few limits on capital account flows. Currently, many see only the negative aspects of these moves, but capital account liberalization in Indonesia could not have been timed differently: this was a period in which the Indonesia government needed foreign capital to invest in infrastructure and local companies. These capital inflows greatly contributed to the rapid rates of growth in Indonesia at that time. However, the Indonesian case does demonstrate that there may be a need for greater administrative control over capital flows. The actions taken to open Indonesia to greater inflows of capital should have been complemented by additional policy changes.

Currently, India's policies concerning capital inflows are favorably contrasted with those in Indonesia. In India, restrictions on capital flows have long been in place. However, India registered much lower rates of economic growth during the 1970s and 1980s than Indonesia, in part due to lower inflows of foreign capital. Only now do these controls appear to be to India's advantage; previously this was not the case.

The crisis in Indonesia began in early July 1997. Because of increased volatility and the reactions of investors in the currency markets, attitudes toward emerging markets changed and words like "chaos" and "contagion" began to be used. International financial publications also started to examine the capital flows into Malaysia, Indonesia, the Philippines, and South Korea. Capital inflows into the region totaled $93 billion in 1996 but shifted to an outflow of more than $12 billion in 1997.

Domestic institutions could not cope with the shocks. A falling currency signaled the beginnings of problems, but the initial response in Indonesia was to continue the previous policy of a pegged exchange rate traded within a band. The band within which the rupiah traded against the dollar was widened, but otherwise exchange-rate policy remained the same. However, pressure on the rupiah did not abate. Soon the central bank was forced to intervene on the exchange-rate markets to keep the rupiah within the official trading band.

Next, monetary policy was tightened. Then the crisis began shifting to other sectors of the economy. A domino effect quickly developed as the weakening rupiah affected the institutionally weak banking sector. Relations between Indonesian banks and corresponding banks abroad worsened. The subsequent loss of confidence in the banking sector was severe as sixteen insolvent banks were closed. When a bank owned by one of President Suharto's sons and another owned by a close relative both closed, the seriousness of the situation was better understood. Investors reasoned that if a bank controlled by these close Suharto associates could be closed, other banks would be hit as well. The loss of confidence in the banking sector and the rupiah soon spread to private businesses on the fear that they would default on short-term debt payments. As interest rates were raised, domestic entities were squeezed. An acute need developed to address policies toward the real sector.

As the economy deteriorated, the contagion spread to the social and political sectors. The policy response of the government was to attempt to prop up confidence in the economy. The best way to accomplish this was by requesting the assistance of the IMF. In late October 1997, the government invited the IMF to begin talks, which led to the implementation of a standby agreement. The core of the IMF program in Indonesia was a comprehensive policy package designed to deal with the insolvent banks, improve supervision of banks, and attempt to overcome structural rigidity in the real sector of the economy. The essence of the IMF agreement was to create a strong macroeconomic framework in order to improve the current account, including a tight monetary stance as well as a substantial fiscal tightening. The program also in-cluded a comprehensive strategy to restructure the financial sector, in-cluding the closure of financially weak institutions. The third major com-ponent incorporated a broad range of structural measures that would help to improve the operations of the government.

Although problems developed quite quickly, stabilization has been slow. The policy of closing insolvent banks, intended to raise confidence in the banking sector, actually damaged it further. Once the banking sector was damaged, the economy began to deteriorate. The linchpin of the crisis was the collapse of the banking sector. The weak banking system constrained the monetary authority in conducting monetary policy and banking supervision, as well as facilitating payment sys-tems. The dilemma is how to deal with weak banks. Raising interest rates to strengthen the domestic currency may not help weak institu-tions. The inclusion of banking soundness as an explicit objective of monetary policy may be in order.

Delay in making key policy decisions was an especially costly char-acteristic of the Indonesian crisis. The sooner the problem banks are identified, the sooner the problems can be resolved and the less costly is the resolution of the problems. Since policymakers waited so long to address the situation, the cost of fixing the problems grew substantially and it became more difficult to address the issues. As lender of last resort, early on the Indonesian central bank actually acted in opposi-tion to what needed to be done to support the economy. Instead of clos-ing weak financial institutions, it supported these banks. There was no motivation to close a bad bank while the economy was doing fine because the weak institution could probably limp along if the economy remained in good shape. Even though there is an increasingly appar-ent link between banking soundness and economic strength, many of the banking systems in Southeast Asia are simply not yet strong enough. The monetary authorities in emerging markets are ill prepared by international economic organizations to deal with monetary crises. This lack of preparation had a devastating impact on Indonesia and South Korea.

Monetary policy issues are typically short-term when compared with larger, long-term problems of banking restructuring. Tight or loose mon-etary policy is a short-term issue. On the other hand, banking restruc-turing deals with problems of efficiency, management, supervision, reg-ulation, and law enforcement, which are medium- or long-term issues. When a package of policies needs to be created, it is difficult to create a single set of short-term and long-term solutions because the problems to be addressed include both micro- and macroeconomic issues. In a package, those labels are moot because they must be linked. Although the Indonesian central bank could not close down a number of insolvent banks quickly, it could make real reductions in tariffs to encourage imports. Policy measures aimed at restructuring the banking sector must be completed in stages. When public impressions are fragile, the closure of insolvent banks, although necessary for the creation of a sound banking system, may actually further lower the confidence of the public. Nonetheless, although it is a challenge, banks should be closed as soon as possible. The sooner a bank is closed, once the economy can bear such a closure, the less costly it is to the economy as a whole.

In short, some lessons regarding financial liberalization can be learned from the Indonesian liberalization process. Banking liberalization must be conducted in conjunction with an improvement of the financial infrastructure, including proper regulations and strict prudential measures, adequate disclosure, solid corporate governance, legal protection, and market discipline. Studies have also shown the possible sequencing of financial liberalization. The issue of central bank independence is also important. However, different conditions may require a different sequence.

The IMF therapy is to discipline the public sector, but the most severe problems remain in the private sector in Indonesia. The government must return to these issues and consider them more fully. Within this context, private debt must be addressed because the remaining problems are quite severe. However, some tentative steps have been taken in the right direction. To stop the downslide, Indonesia needs to convince international observers and investors that things have turned around.

A great deal of discussion has focused on the creeping devaluation of the rupiah and the necessity of locating financing abroad. It is not valid to say that the players in the market always know better than the authorities or always act with foresight. Business leaders invested in a very speculative manner, and instead of hedging their investments, they financed their debts with foreign currency and relied on the creeping devaluation and the widening of the exchange-rate band to ensure affordable repayment. When the rupiah was freely floated, businesses were exposed.

Like Bulgarian authorities, the Indonesian authorities examined the idea of implementing a currency board to resolve the crisis. The was first broached in the early days of the crisis, when it was unclear what could be done to end the crisis. However, the debate became public in the first quarter of 1998 when the crisis was in full bloom.

Too many economic problems still stand in the way of the institution of a currency board in Indonesia. The rupiah would have been strengthened by a stroke of the pen if a currency board had been adopted, but little would have been done to improve confidence in the banking sector. Indonesian reserves were also unlikely to be substantial enough to support the base money required to run the currency board. A number of requirements needed to be fulfilled before a currency board could have been installed. As a result of crony capitalism and individuals' close links with the government, the private sector was much more powerful than the state sector. A strong system of business ethics was also missing. Because of these economic weaknesses, a currency board would have been very difficult to implement and sustain.

Exchange Rates: When to Fix and When to Float?

HONG KONG AND THE PEOPLE'S REPUBLIC OF CHINA

Two years ago, it seemed clear that the Hong Kong Monetary Authority (HKMA) and the People's Bank of China (PBC) were converging into a type of central bank broadly similar to those emerging in most developing countries. The characteristics of this type of central bank include 100 percent backing of its monetary liabilities in the form of foreign assets. These banks typically enjoy limited autonomy to undertake market operations with domestic securities. Their function of serving as lender of last resort to deposit-taking institutions is quite limited and well defined. Finally, there is a clear commitment to exchange-rate stability, including a rule that pegs the domestic currency to a foreign currency or a basket of foreign currencies. Although the HKMA and the PBC would continue to show important differences in how each enforced the policies listed above, the differences were expected to become less acute as long as the Chinese government remained committed to transforming the PBC into a modern central bank.

Today, both the HKMA and the PBC remain committed to a fixed exchange rate, the significant differences in their institutional frameworks notwithstanding. However, neither commitment is credible.

In Hong Kong, the economic fundamentals have changed radically, and a serious disequilibrium in relative prices must be corrected. Strong comparisons can be made to the crisis in Chile in the early 1970s. There, asset prices were so high that some sort of change was needed. They have declined by 50 to 60 percent in Hong Kong, but this decline may not be enough. Real wages remain a concern as well. The HKMA has some discretionary right to intervene in the market, but it is limited even though it does not act as a currency board.

The situation in China is quite different. The economic fundamentals are not sound because China remains a transitional economy. Slow progress in reforming the state sector threatens the high growth rates of the past twenty years, and recent developments in the world economy have weakened the demand for Chinese goods. The state sector remains very large, both in terms of enterprises and in terms of the banking system. The problems of the Chinese banking sector are similar to those of Indonesia, but the problems are worse in China because some of the banks are so large. The lack of a strong banking sector encourages the proliferation of bad loans: there are no checks in place to prevent them, and officials insist on supporting nonperforming state-owned enterprises.

The choice of an exchange-rate regime should be based on long-term considerations about the integration of each economy into the world economy and the economy's adjustment mechanisms to shocks. Hong Kong cannot become a world financial center with a weak currency. To be integrated into the world economy, Hong Kong can follow one of two models: the "New York" model or the "Singapore" model. Under the "New York" model, Hong Kong would continue to provide a number of services, but the city would not have its own currency. The "Singapore" model allows for the introduction of industrial policies, and the HKMA would have to follow a monetary policy that would grant some discretionary power to the bank. To integrate most completely into the world economy, Hong Kong would be better off without a currency of its own.

In China, a number of barriers to the internal movement of labor and capital continue to exist. The country needs to choose an exchange-rate regime that provides some flexibility for daily transactions, given the size of the country. However, China lacks a high degree of credibility. As a result, the PBC cannot possess too much discretion within this increased flexibility. A free-floating currency is only a theory; if a floating rate is to be adopted, China needs to introduce some sort of more restrictive fiscal policy.

The end result of a transition to a new exchange-rate regime greatly depends on how the transition is handled. If Hong Kong moves to a "New York" model, the process will be smooth as long as the consequences of a rapid dollarization of the economy are accepted. If Hong Kong chooses to shift to the "Singapore" model instead, the transition will largely depend on the consistency of all the policy changes involved in this choice. For China, the transition will depend on the foreign-exchange market conditions at the time the new exchange-rate regime is introduced. The PBC is also very committed to a fixed-exchange-rate policy in order to protect Hong Kong in case China changes its own exchange-rate policy. For both countries, changes in monetary policy need to be consistent with foreign-exchange market conditions. This is a lesson that has not been learned well by Latin Americans.

HUNGARY

In Hungary, all of the functions served by the exchange rate are quite important because of the disequilibria inherited from before 1989. Exports are quite a significant component of the Hungarian economy. Despite the fact that the Hungarian forint has been appreciating in real effective terms, growth in exports remained high as a result of increases in efficiency.

The main reasons for the growth of inflation in Hungary are domestic. Many argue that inflation has been caused by the rapid growth in wages. However, others contend that inflation is more closely linked to the fiscal deficit and the changes in the price system, including distortions inherited from the previous system. As a result, exchange-rate policy can only partially curb inflation.

During the transition, two exchange-rate regimes have been in place in Hungary. From 1990 to 1995, the forint was tied to a basket of currencies by an adjustable peg. During that period, the forint was devalued twenty-two times, for a total devaluation of 87 percent. The National Bank of Hungary, the Hungarian central bank, was continually forced to fight against speculation regarding devaluation. At the same time, the real effective exchange rate appreciated. This regime was directed at curbing inflation rather than improving competitiveness. During this time, export growth was relatively weak.

In March 1995, a crawling peg was introduced. The rate of crawl was publicly announced, and this action helped to defuse devaluation rumors. As mentioned before, high growth in efficiency continued to push exports. The crawling peg was introduced along with other austerity measures, including a one-off devaluation and an 8 percent import surcharge that lasted until the summer of 1997. The crawling peg eventually led to a real appreciation of the forint, and the government was forced to attract portfolio investment, which helped to strengthen the forint. By 1997, it was no longer necessary to cover the current account deficit with investment inflows, and direct foreign investment could slow.

The crawling peg reinforced the fundamentals of economic policy and the competitiveness of the Hungarian economy. In addition, it helped to lower inflation. However, the fear of falling domestic interest rates remains because of the potential to damage household savings.

The dominant view regarding the future of the exchange-rate regime is that the crawling peg will need to be maintained for as long as inflation remains drastically different from world inflation rates. The current challenge is the need to stop the capital outflow from the country. Foreign investors are selling their investments and reducing their portfolios. Stock prices on the Hungarian exchange have lost 50 percent of their value. The forint has fallen from the stronger side of the band as of late, and the central bank has been forced to intervene regularly.

The short-term economic outlook for Hungary is mixed. Moderate capital outflows are expected to continue, but they should slow. As a result, there will be no need for special intervention. However, if the rapid rate of capital outflow continues for an extended period of time, foreign-exchange reserves ($9 billion) and bond portfolio and foreign-equity portfolios ($2 billion), although significant, may be drawn down. Foreigners have sold over 50 percent of their holdings of Hungarian government bonds, a fall in foreign holdings from 400 billion forints to about 200 billion forints. Although foreigners have fled both the bond and the equity markets, the banking sector and macroeconomic fundamentals remain quite strong. As a result, the flight of foreign capital is difficult to explain, but foreign investors may be covering their losses in other emerging markets.

On the downside, the country's risk might rise, making the country less attractive to investors. If domestic investors' confidence collapses and a shift from forint deposits to dollar deposits begins, emergency measures may be required. The first step of such measures would likely include a significant increase in interest rates.

Chapter 5

The Creation of Sound Banking Systems

In light of the Asian crisis and the rocky transition experience of several Southeast European countries, observers have concluded that the creation of a strong banking sector is a significant prerequisite for long-term financial stability. Financial crisis is always detrimental to economic performance, but it appears clear that the impact of the recent crises was more severe in countries with weak banking structures and limited financial infrastructures than in countries with more sound foundations. This conference session examined the programs under way to help rebuild the Thai economy, with particular emphasis on the bank recapitalization scheme, and discussed how Slovenia has successfully worked through problems in its banking system.

Thailand

Although Thailand was the first to fall into crisis in Southeast Asia, it is not clear that Thailand will be the first to regain the confidence of international investors and recover. One of the most important steps to regain investor confidence will be to send investors a signal that Thailand's reform program for the financial sector is working and, in particular, that the reform of corporate governance is moving forward. The World Bank feels that Thailand has come quite far as a result of its stabilization program; capital began to return in January and February 1998. However, despite the fact that Thailand was doing all of the right things, capital inflows were curtailed again when it became clear that the problems in Japan were more serious and fundamental than anyone had suspected.

A few key rates stabilized during 1997–98. Following the June 1997 decision to remove the baht from its peg of 25 to the dollar, the baht fell to almost 32 in July 1997. In June 1997, the overnight repo rate, the rate that sets the trend for the rest of the interest rates, began to climb. It rose from 9.8 percent in March 1997 to 17.0 percent in June 1997. The commercial bank lending rate had started to rise, but the overall interest rate structure seemed reasonable. However, the overnight repo rate climbed to 24.0 percent in December 1997 at the height of the crisis. At this point, the crisis of confidence about Thailand merged with the crisis of confidence about the region as a whole. Thailand then slid into a very serious decline. The stock market index also showed considerable weaknesses.

The exchange rate has improved a great deal and in September 1998 stabilized at around 41 baht to the dollar. However, some of the most significant variables, including real GDP growth, remain troublesome. The World Bank estimated that GDP would fall an estimated 7.0 percent in 1998, after falling 0.4 percent in 1997. Growth was projected to return in 1999, with GDP growing by 0.5 percent. Consumption dropped by 10 percent in the first nine months of 1998 and investment in 1998 was off by nearly 30 percent compared with 1997. These numbers are anchored in the region-wide crisis that Thailand is facing.

On the upside, Thailand has done well in managing its external debt. The short-term debt-to-gross reserves ratio has improved significantly, totaling 155 in 1998. This ratio indicates the amount of short-term debt outstanding that exceeds reserves. The ratio was projected to deteriorate to almost 300 in 1999, provided the Japanese banking system held together. The extent to which short-term debt will become a serious problem has everything to do with the Japanese banks' decisions to keep rolling over their loans to Japanese corporations operating in Thailand. If Japan begins to pull back its loans, as feared, it could cause quite a problem.

A very remarkable turnaround of the current account has occurred. The story here should be of considerable concern to the developed world. The current account surplus of 11 billion baht in 1997 was caused by a fierce reduction in imports. The goal of the World Bank program was for economic turnaround to be driven by increased exports. Thai exports remain flat. Adjustment through reduced imports rather than increased exports lies at the core of the recovery problem not only in Thailand but throughout Southeast Asia.

The stabilization program put into place by the IMF was created at a time when it was not clear that Japan would be suffering from its current difficulties and that the world economy would be in trouble. Instead, the IMF hoped that a short, sharp shock would help to ease Thailand's problems. The initial analysis concluded that Thailand was suffering from too much investment, especially inflows of portfolio investment. The capital market had received huge capital inflows between 1990 and 1996, in the form both of foreign direct investment and of portfolio investment. As a result, it was hoped that after the devaluation, investment could be rechanneled into areas where it was productive rather than into unproductive areas such as real estate. The money supply was sharply limited, which resulted in a sharp increase in interest rates. In turn, rising interest rates would have an impact on people's investment decisions. Accompanying this program was a fiscal policy to limit deficits because it was understood that there would be costs to financial sector restructuring. These costs would be met by the public surpluses that would arise. Since the global crisis deepened, many of these policies have been revised, including the fiscal and monetary policy stances, which are both much looser now.

In addition to the financial sector stabilization program was a program for structural reform aimed at the financial sector. In the summer of 1997, Thailand had ninety-two finance companies, which accounted for almost 18 percent of the assets of the financial sector. Many of these companies lent to sectors with a great deal of excess capacity, so the actual rate of return on these investments was too low to service the loans. To compound matters, some of the lending decisions were motivated by political rather than financial reasons. However, the precipitating event that triggered the collapse of these finance companies was the devaluation of the baht. In Thailand, as in Indonesia, finance companies had borrowed in foreign currencies. The companies then relent in baht. When the baht fell, the finance companies' domestic assets were much lower in value than the foreign liabilities they had incurred to make their loans. As a result, finance companies ran into serious trouble. The government decided to suspend the operations of forty-two of the finance companies, almost 10 percent of the total financial sector.

The suspension of the financial companies led to a protracted policy debate on what to do with these businesses because it was difficult for the government to take resolute action in the summer of 1997. With a relatively weak governing coalition, it was especially hard for the government to enforce the closure of the companies and banks of several of its important supporters.

In November 1997, a new government took power and was able to make decisions resolutely. At last, in June 1998, fifty-six of the fifty-eight finance companies that had been suspended were closed. Next, the government had to decide what to do with the remaining assets, totaling nearly one trillion baht, without further damaging the market. Many of the closed financial companies were closely tied to banks. Currently, eight privately owned banks and about thirty financial companies remain open.

The government was confronted with the need to put a public recapitalization program in place for the banks that remained open. This project too had serious political ramifications. Many began to realize that the government's program to bail out the financial sector was costing the government a significant amount of money. The moral hazard associated with any decision to use public funds to recapitalize banks is that the banks may decide not to do anything until the government reveals its plans and may thus increase the fiscal cost of such bailouts.

The recapitalization scheme devised by the government attempts to motivate private investment into the financial institutions, which will also receive some public funds. This is the first tier of the scheme. The agreement will provide cash to the banks in return for equity, provided that there is a similar amount of cash coming from private foreign investment. The second tier of the recapitalization scheme involves the provision of government debt instruments in exchange for "bad" loans so as to improve the balance sheets of the banks. The debt instruments will be provided only if these institutions engage in debt restructuring with their debtors. The goal is not only to provide support to financial institutions but, through these institutions, to rescue the whole corporate sector.

The recapitalization scheme was announced on August 15, 1998, and the details are still being worked out. The actual amount of capital required will evolve as more and more banks decide to take advantage of the scheme. The market fears that it may be difficult to get recalcitrant banks to take advantage of these schemes because the banks are afraid to lose control, especially the many banks dominated by powerful families. How to motivate recalcitrant banks to participate is an issue that must be addressed as the scheme evolves.

The recapitalization program alone will not be enough. It may provide the banks with the cushion that they need to restart lending, but at the same time, mechanisms must be in place to bring Thai corporate debtors to the table so that workouts can be negotiated. Right now, almost one-third of Thai corporations are suffering severe financial problems and are unable to meet even their interest payments on outstanding debts. Preferably, out-of-court, informal agreements could be developed, since formal, court-arranged workouts are both expensive and time-consuming. To promote workouts, strong bankruptcy and foreclosure laws must be put into place so that creditors can enforce foreclosure on reluctant debtors. This will require a large shift in the legal culture in Thailand because debtors are rarely taken to court. Right now, the Thai legal culture is one in which the parties compromise and hope that problems will be worked out over time.

The incentive to change is to be provided by the recapitalization scheme. Institutions that are actively engaged in discussions with their debtors will receive additional capital from the government. In addition, a credit crunch and a reluctance to lend have appeared, resulting in serious corporate sector difficulties. The credit crunch has been caused by the reluctance of banks to lend. This reluctance is due in part to a lack of transparency in the way that accounts are kept and the way that loan applications are made. For example, it is very difficult to learn if an applicant who claims to be using a loan to engage in export is actually using the loan for that purpose rather than servicing a real estate loan. Thailand liberalized its capital account and financial system very quickly but did not put the proper regulatory framework into place as the system was liberalized.

A second incentive to restructure involves some forbearance in how quickly companies are required to contend with losses on their balance sheets. Those financial institutions that receive cash from the government will be required to make 100 percent provisioning against "bad" loans immediately, that is, they must completely write off any loans for which they request government assistance. This means that more capital to improve the balance sheets of the banks will be needed than can be lent out. However, there is some forbearance on this prudential regulation for companies that engage in corporate debt restructuring; in these cases, provisioning can be stretched out over a five-year period.

The tax code also needs to be revised, along with the entire area of corporate governance, including disclosure of information. The tax code treats forgiven debt as a windfall gain and taxes it in the highest bracket. Fairly substantial reforms must be made in the way that accounting is performed. Here also, substantial progress has been made.

The Thai response to the Asian crisis was one of the region's most aggressive. Thailand was initially in denial about the seriousness of the economic crisis, but the Thais quickly decided to roll up their sleeves and jump in to do the work that needed to be done. Indonesia was different because the government initially became mired in blaming someone else for its difficulties. As a result, Indonesia remains in a very vulnerable position. In addition, the government in Indonesia does not enjoy the same level of support as does the Thai government. Malaysia continues to blame others. The situation in Malaysia is quite unfortunate because the economy is very small and extremely dependent on foreign direct investment.

The macroeconomic fundamentals in Thailand look fine. If Thailand were the only country in crisis, the market would have seen these signals as significant cues to resume lending. However, Thailand is in recession at a time when all of the other countries in the region are also in recession and when there is talk of a global contagion effect. As a result, Thailand will have to contend with at least one more year of anemic growth in 1999.

Slovenia

Slovenia undertook a very cautious approach to financial reform and has never been under the scrutiny of the IMF or other international groups. The power in parliament is quite dispersed, forcing Slovenia to institute reformist policies more gradually rather than repeating the mistakes made by other countries that reformed more quickly. In addition, Slovenia had the highest level of economic development among countries in the region because of its openness to the West during the socialist era. Slovenia is also home to a strong middle class, and the economic policy of "self-management" has provided a firm base for privatization because the new owners had already been active in the companies and were interested in future success.

The general performance of the economy is quite good. However, it is not yet clear if this performance can be continued in light of a global slowdown and the threat of the spread of the crisis to Central Europe. Although Slovenia enjoys the best credit rating among transition countries, it cannot sustain its international competitiveness without reforms. Value-added tax will be introduced in July 1999 at a rate of 19 percent, but Slovenia must still undertake pension reform. Privatization is lagging, and capital markets are still underdeveloped. Although the first round of privatization has ended, corporate governance remains weak and the state-owned sector continues to produce almost 50 percent of Slovenian GDP. State aid to enterprises and agriculture should become more transparent. Conditions for foreign direct investment should be liberalized, and regulations concerning treatment of foreign investors need to be fully implemented. Since 25 percent of prices are still controlled by the government, prices must still be fully liberalized. It is expected that outside pressure from the EU will be of significant help to push some of these reforms through the Slovenian parliament.

Slovenia started with a floating exchange rate because its independence was not initially recognized internationally and the country lacked foreign-exchange reserves in order to institute a fixed exchange rate. This exchange-rate regime has remained in place. However, the tolar appreciated nominally vis-à-vis both the dollar and the deutsche mark in 1998, leading analysts to question whether the Slovenian national currency is overvalued. In June 1998, the Bank of Slovenia intervened on the foreign-exchange market, and this caused the tolar's appreciation to decelerate.

With the exception of Slovenia, all of the current Central European frontrunners for EU membership have undergone banking crises. The three Baltic states, Hungary, and Poland had banking crises in the early 1990s. Romanian banks suffered when the economy nearly collapsed in 1997. In the Czech Republic, thirteen banks failed in 1996. Bulgaria's banking system all but collapsed in 1997 as a result of fraudulent lending. Slovakia's third-largest bank was bailed out by the National Bank of Slovakia in December 1997.

Slovenia managed to restructure and develop its banking system without larger problems. The new government was able to apply Western rehabilitation approaches used in the United States and Spain because Slovenia is wealthy enough to spend budget funds on the capitalization of shattered banks. In poorer emerging markets, which have no funds available for such uses, the banks must first be privatized; restructuring is left to the new, and often foreign, owners.

The experience of bank restructuring in Slovenia was unique because in no other country where bank rehabilitation had been undertaken had an attempt been made to rehabilitate more than 50 percent of the banking sector at once. The Bank Rehabilitation Agency was founded in Slovenia in 1991. The agency supervised the banks in rehabilitation, managed bad assets, and serviced government bonds swapped for bad assets of banks. Bank rehabilitation included seven main objectives:

1. Replenishing the capital of the banks to meet standards of the Bank for International Settlements
2. Streamlining and consolidating the banks' operations, thereby reducing staff and operating expenses and improving their future potential earnings
3. Fostering competition
4. Building positive cash flows and current operating incomes
5. Reducing banking interest rates
6. Regaining credibility in international financial markets
7. Introducing basic principles of prudential behavior by banks

Slow but robust growth helped Slovenia to avoid a banking collapse. The Slovenian banking system is relatively healthy, but it is not yet competitive. The number of banks has remained stable as of late. It doubled from 1990 to 1992 but fell by one bank per year in 1995–97. In 1997, the average return on banking equity was 7.1 percent.

Restructuring the banking sector was relatively successful. Bad assets were swapped for government bonds totaling 6 to 8 percent of GDP. Three banks successfully launched self-rehabilitation. The results of rehabilitation were largely positive. Although Slovenian public debt grew to 1.8 billion deutsche marks, this amount has been partially lowered through the recovery of bad loans and in 1998 totaled less than 10 percent of GDP. The share of bad assets in the banking sector fell from 10 percent to less than 4 percent of total loans while the share of A-classified loans grew from less than 80 percent to 89 percent. The banking sector posted $110 million in aggregate profits in 1995 after a trend of continued losses. The share of banking sector assets for the banks in rehabilitation was reduced from 50 percent to 40 percent. However, their capital totaled 850 million deutsche marks, up from a negative capital of 1,500 million deutsche marks before rehabilitation. Banks in rehabilitation also posted profits above the average of the entire sector, demonstrating improved institutional performance and much enhanced management of human resources. In June 1997, the rehabilitation of banks was formally completed.

Today, the restructured banks are among the strongest banks in Slovenia. One, Nova Ljubljanska Banka, is currently being prepared for privatization, and it is hoped that foreign investors will be involved in the sale. The bank is by far the largest in Slovenia, with a 28 percent share of the market. It is now adequately capitalized, has introduced sufficient provisioning, and has implemented sound lending policies and cost-control measures. In addition, an efficient organizational structure and highly motivated management team are in place. The bank has also developed an international network with five affiliates and eight representative offices in major financial centers of the world. Utilizing its own experiences, the bank is also offering technical assistance to banks currently under rehabilitation in Croatia and Macedonia.

The first banking law was quite restrictive, but only one bank went bankrupt. Now, natural consolidation is under way. The new banking law, which took four years to write, is an attempt to approach EU standards, although it is not yet in line with them. Since EU membership will not likely occur for Slovenia before 2005, there is still time to iron out the remaining differences.

There is some regulation of foreign investment in the banking industry. Currently, only five Slovenian banks are majority-owned by foreigners, but thirteen are under foreign joint ownership, representing 18 and 46 percent of all banks, respectively. Surprisingly, foreign banks have not come to Slovenia to use the country as a window to former Yugoslavia, as had been anticipated. Instead, foreign banks have tended to follow trade flows. Since Slovenia is a relatively small country, it has not attracted a great deal of attention from foreign banks. The core business of foreign banks in Slovenia is the collection of deposits and international payments. Loans to corporate customers and individuals by these banks compose only a small share of their overall business, although the share of this business has grown in recent years. The major reason for the very conservative lending policy of foreign banks is insufficient legal protection of creditors.

Chapter 6

Foreign Investment as Solution and Problem

As the global economic crisis widens, parts of the "Washington Consensus" are now being reconsidered. Although openness is generally considered welfare-enhancing, it carries requirements that must be met if welfare gains are to be maximized and the costs of openness are to be minimized. The costs of openness can be quite high if these requirements are not met. Because of the failure to satisfy these requirements in a number of emerging markets, limits on capital flows are now being considered. The failure of policymakers to ensure that these requirements are met has been a key reason for the Russian crisis. Commentators have argued that the foreign actors contributed to the crisis because of moral hazards created by past IMF rescues. There is strong evidence that fund managers, fully aware that Russia was headed for serious economic problems, moved money from Southeast Asia into Russia. However, all assumed that Western governments and international financial institutions would rescue Russia and shield investors from losses. In actuality, investors have suffered considerable losses following the devaluation of the ruble. Nonetheless, the role of large flows in and out of portfolio investments in emerging markets and the role of the IMF as a lender of last resort for these countries have precipitated a policy debate about the value of international capital flows and IMF programs.

Global Capital Flows

Some of Russia's problems are due to its approach to international capital flows. Russia's limited restructuring favored shorter-term foreign portfolio investment. In contrast, Hungary pursued more extensive privatization and foreign direct investment. Although there are different ways to open a country to foreign capital, structural reforms need to address certain prerequisites. The capital markets have gone wrong in confusing exchange-rate stability for structural reform. Any reworking of the "Washington Consensus" needs to take this factor into account.

In Hungary's case, openness has given it the strongest banking system in Central Europe and a very firm export base. Both promise to deliver solid, sustainable growth in living standards over the medium term. This did not happen overnight. Decisive and costly steps had to be taken to get to this point. Near the beginning of the transition, Hungary began a painful restructuring and closed down a number of enterprises in the state sector, thus providing a stronger sense of credibility concerning financial stabilization. At the root of its current success was a decision by the Hungarian government to intensify structural reforms as investors began to lose faith in global capital markets around the time of the Mexican crisis in 1995–96. The government accelerated privatization and used the proceeds to reduce public debt. Most saleable Hungarian firms have now been sold, and many of those that could not be sold have been closed. Although the sector of the economy that has benefited from foreign investment is growing, the rest of the economy is not performing as well. Some reforms are still needed. The present government is now struggling with some of the political fallout from these earlier efforts. There is still much to be done on tax and health care reform. The size and cost of the state sector remains a problem.

Russia never bit the bullet. Russia privatized the easy way, mainly to insiders. This move continued the financial indiscipline that had become widely entrenched in the economy. Insider privatization has ensured a lack of restructuring at the enterprise level, in contrast to privatization in Poland and Hungary. Bankruptcy provisions have been nonexistent in Russia, and the banks were poorly supervised in times of financial instability and speculation. Russian banks, developed as speculative vehicles, have had a tough time turning into banks able to allocate credit efficiently on the basis of good risk management. Russia was open to portfolio inflows but not to inflows of foreign direct investment, especially in the energy sector, where the interest of foreign investors would have been the strongest. Portfolio investment helped the authorities to temporarily finance unsustainable fiscal deficits that were caused by insufficient structural reform. Now, what is seen is the wreckage caused by the unraveling of this type of stabilization policy. The limited restructuring did not meet the requirements of open capital markets. Initially, Russia benefited from a sharp drop in interest rates and less pressure on a difficult fiscal situation, but this lasted for only a short while. When foreign investors left, the entire financial system collapsed.

Openness does call for painful structural reforms, but it can also have benefits. The issue is whether capital will flow into a country that is open. The process of transformation to a market economy usually introduces a high level of inflation in the short run. In Asia, the process of exchange-rate adjustment and some of the structural reforms in the banking sector have had a similar effect. Once growth is stable, declining inflation will make local equity and bond markets attractive to foreign portfolio investors, especially if they are able to judge that the fiscal adjustments necessary to deal with budgetary pressures in the early stages of the transformation are likely to be sustainable. If the fiscal adjustments can be maintained, then domestic interest rates will decline and the exchange rate will become stable over the medium term. Fiscal adjustments require structural reforms, but these must be introduced over time. When these changes have not been introduced in a timely manner, a period of instability can follow, as has been seen in the Czech Republic.

There may possibly be an economic slowdown in 1999 and some changes in the political cycle in Central Europe. For example, some factions in Hungary are arguing for an increase in the fiscal deficit. Expectations of looser fiscal policy may help explain some of the weakening that has been seen in Central European currencies recently. It is not only the crisis in Russia that is worrisome but also the long-term effects of the Russian crisis on Hungary and Poland.

These types of near-term instabilities make openness important in another way. The opening to short-term foreign borrowing in Russia, coupled with an exchange rate that was not as fixed as it appeared to be, proved quite painful. Hungary, in emphasizing privatization, never opened to short-term capital inflows in the same way as Russia but laid the groundwork for the openness that is necessary for medium-term economic investment. A majority of the short-term foreign capital inflows that have gone into Hungary have gone into the stock exchange, where their ability to put pressure on the exchange rate is necessarily more limited because losses are first incurred on equity prices. Privatization attracted foreign equity investment, which is an important way of getting capital inflows to finance imports and to cover current account deficits. Privatization also lays the basis for ongoing inflows of capital as the subsidiaries created through privatization receive further investment from parent companies or banks linked to parent companies.

Since many investors assumed that Russia was too big or too nuclear to fail, little attention was paid to how flows went into Russia. If the exchange rate is unstable, investors will usually suffer losses. If the stock market is overvalued, an investor can also expect losses. Both of these conditions existed in Russia.

There are different ways to open a country to foreign capital, and there are clear requirements that structural reforms need to address. These necessary reforms are not inconsistent with the "Washington Consensus." On portfolio flows, the question is whether policies are likely to be credible and sustainable over the medium term. Where the capital markets may have gone wrong was in confusing exchange-rate stability for structural reform. Any intellectual revision of the consensus needs to accommodate this experience.

Southeast Europe

Although most of the transition countries have liberalized their economies, governments in Southeast Europe continue to maintain barriers and restrictions—some externally imposed, some self-imposed, and some inherited. The consequence has been that the region has continued to experience trade and other real and policy-induced shocks. These shocks have motivated most, though not all, of the states in the region to advance on the path either of regional integration or of European integration. Because the EU has conditioned further European integration for countries in Southeast Europe on more regional integration, the level and development of regional trade integration should become an important institutional and policy issue in Southeast Europe. However, there has been little regional integration thus far. The failure of these countries to integrate both regionally and into the global economy has been an enormous loss to their potential development.

The population of Southeast Europe, including Greece, totals 70 million. However, the aggregate GDP of the region is only slightly higher than Austria's, home to only 8 million people. Without Greece, Southeast Europe produces only as much as Greece, though Southeast Europe has three times more people. However, Greece exports only slightly more than Slovenia and not much more than some larger economies in Southeast Europe. Thus, the largest economy in the region does not stimulate foreign trade in the region. As a consequence, regional trade is not expected to increase or act as a decisive influence on the growth of output in the region.

There is very little interregional trade. Countries in Southeast Europe trade more with Germany and other EU countries than with each other. Southeast Europe is an extreme case of illiberal trade. The governments have used trade barriers as a source of revenue; internal integration in terms of what can be traded across borders is very limited.

Geographic proximity in Southeast Europe has not led to increased regional trade under more open trading conditions. For some countries, neighbors are not trading partners. For instance, Slovenia and Croatia trade with each other and with Macedonia and sell to Bosnia-Herzegovina, but they do not trade significantly with other countries in Southeast Europe. Here, historical factors play a significant role both in the persistence of some trade between the former Yugoslav republics and in its absence with non-Yugoslav states. The low level of trade integration with other Balkan countries is due to political and economic divisions during the socialist era. For almost no Southeast European country is another Southeast European country the main trading partner. Though the region plays a more important role for some countries—notably Bosnia-Herzegovina and perhaps Macedonia—trade with the EU is more important by far.

The institutional impediments to trade in Southeast Europe are quite severe. Security problems caused by the disintegration of Yugoslavia, the events in Albania, and the war in Bosnia have placed huge constraints on economic development. The current crisis in Kosovo demonstrates that the problems will not be solved at any point in the near future. Many of the countries suffer from macroeconomic instability. The transformation to a market economy has been largely incomplete. The most extreme case is Yugoslavia, where some of the changes have actually been retrograde; in other countries, such as Romania, the changes simply got "stuck." Regional protectionism exists because countries have very limited official economic relations with one another. Black marketeering remains a huge part of daily life. The low level of rule of law outside of Slovenia and Macedonia is also not conducive to investment.

As a result, there are very few assets in which foreign investors may safely invest in these countries. The fact that integration into the world economy has been postponed means that the countries that are now trying to attract foreign investment are latecomers to international capital markets. Unfortunately, now is not the time to liberalize capital markets because the atmosphere in international capital markets has changed for the worse. With the more difficult international financial climate, many countries have postponed decisions to attract foreign investment even if investment might be beneficial.

With the exception of Bulgaria and Slovenia, these countries run very large current account deficits. As a result, they need inflows on the capital account. Although the countries are not integrated into the world capital market, in this instance it would be better if they were. These countries may be able to escape the Asian crisis, but the actual historical loss due to the failure of these countries to integrate into the global economy is enormous. There are few prospects for the future integration of these countries into the rest of Europe. There will be little in the way of an outside push to transform the economies. For other transition countries, the desire to join the EU has forced them to reform faster than would otherwise have been the case, but in Southeast Europe even those countries with better-than-average transition records are likely to enjoy limited investment and limited integration with the EU. This situation is conducive to the development and implementation of counterproductive policies.

Key Regional Investors

GERMANY

Foreign direct investment (FDI) is helpful to these countries, especially in regard to current account deficits. Investment must act as a component that contributes to export growth and helps to rapidly integrate foreign technology into production. At the same time, there must be some sensitivity to local concerns about foreign buyouts of local companies.

At the end of 1997, cumulative FDI in Central and Eastern Europe totaled $50 billion. Of that amount, 90 percent went to four countries: the Czech Republic, Poland, Slovakia, and Hungary. Hungary leads in per capita FDI investment, but total investment has been highest in Poland. Germany quickly took on an active role in the region as investor and trading partner. However, Germany's role as an investor was only marginal compared with its role as a lender (lending DM 70 billion, or $42 billion).

In the 1980s, West German companies began looking for new investment venues and focused first on Spain and Portugal. Ten years later, Eastern Europe opened with cheap, well-educated labor forces as a newly unified Germany needed to further diversify production. The industrial structure of Germany fits these markets closely. Germany has invested DM 20 billion ($12 billion), 25 to 30 percent of FDI, in the region. The Czech Republic, Hungary, and Poland each received approximately 30 percent of total German investment. Only a bit more than 4 percent went to the CIS. Per capita investment is higher for Hungary and the Czech Republic than for Portugal and Spain—around DM 400 per capita for Hungary and the Czech Republic, DM 110 for Slovakia, DM 15 for Turkey, DM 7 for Bulgaria, and DM 4 for Romania. Cumulative German FDI in Central Europe now equals cumulative German FDI in Japan.

Further growth in FDI in Central Europe is dependent on continued reform in politics and economics. The usefulness of FDI varies from country to country, but the motor vehicle sector clearly demonstrates the good use of investment—for example, Volkswagen's investment in the Czech carmaker Skoda Auto and General Motor's decision to build a new Opel plant in Poland. The region has a chance to remain interesting for German investors if the political and economic framework remains secure.

JAPAN

Japanese direct investment will not lead Southeast Asia out of its doldrums, but Japanese FDI will not dry up. Japanese companies continue to invest in the region, although their hope for profits is relatively low. Almost half of Japanese FDI goes to North America while Asia and Europe each receive around 20 percent. In Asia, investment in manufacturing is quite heavy.

The attitude in Southeast Asia toward direct foreign investment has shifted substantially in recent years. The most noteworthy shift has been in South Korea, where President Kim Dae-jung's positive attitude toward FDI, even from Japan, contrasts sharply with the attitudes of previous governments. He believes that FDI is the best means to help turn the economy around. Eighty-seven percent of Koreans now believe that FDI is beneficial to their country. As a result, laws have been modified to allow international investors to operate under the same conditions as Korean companies, which is a very significant policy change.

As a result of the Asian crisis, Japanese companies needed to invest more money in Southeast Asia because their subsidiaries in the region were losing money. Japanese companies were forced to buy the shares of companies established as joint ventures with Southeast Asian companies that later went out of business. Japanese businesses that use local inputs but sell output abroad are actually doing quite well. The favorable exchange rate makes their products very attractive abroad while keeping input prices relatively low. But the number of companies working in these industries is quite limited. For companies that import inputs to manufacture goods for sale on domestic markets, the economic situation is very grim. The outlook for 1998 was worse than in fiscal 1997. In the longer term, the effects of the crisis may fade a bit, but in the short term, the situation is very difficult.

For now, some industries have actually become more attractive to investors. Some solid companies are being sold at bargain-basement prices, allowing investors to forgo the development of greenfield projects with the construction of new factories.

The credit crunch in Japan caused some Japanese companies to withdraw funds from Southeast Asia. This withdrawal may have exacerbated the crisis. Investing abroad is less attractive now that the yen is relatively weak. Some Japanese think that U.S. investors may now enter the market and buy up Southeast Asian companies because U.S. companies have the cash to invest in the region. Japanese investment may become more active if the yen strengthens. The exchange rate is heavily determined by the policies of the Japanese government; and it is difficult to imagine the Japanese economy improving soon, given the government's policies. In 1999–2000, when Japanese investment would be most beneficial for Southeast Asia, it is unlikely that the Japanese will be able or willing to boost investment.

Chapter 7

International Responses to Economic Crises

The final day of the conference began with a keynote speech by David Lipton, at that time Under Secretary for International Affairs for the U.S. Treasury. His speech—"Priorities of U.S. Policy and the Regional Role of International Financial Institutions"—addressed two basic contentions concerning the crisis: that free capital movements between countries are beneficial to the countries involved; and that the origins of the crisis lie in the free flow of capital.

Lipton argued that to some degree, the current economic crisis in Southeast Asia reflects the economic and financial adolescence of these countries and is a stage that they need to move through. Focusing on openness per se avoids some of the key causes of the crisis. There is obviously a need for institutional reforms. The financial system in Indonesia was enormously weak, and the institutional and legal mechanisms were not in place to deal with its frailty. As a result, the rot continued and grew. In Thailand, particularly in the nonbanking sector, many organizations had extremely weak balance sheets. In South Korea, the *chaebols* and the government discouraged inflows of long-term credit and equity financing but simultaneously encouraged banks to borrow short-term and lend long-term. This mismatch in assets and liabilities engendered the current problems, although it was an effective way to control corporations through a small amount of equity. However, solutions to the economic crises go beyond looking for rot in the system. What is more important is to learn whether the weaknesses in the systems can be corrected or whether they are simply inherent.

Some specific mistakes were made in opening capital markets at a time when current account deficits totaled 6 to 8 percent of GDP. Reliance on international capital to finance fiscal deficits makes it incumbent on governments to manage their budgets correctly. Because of pressures from international financial markets, the room for error in the construction of macroeconomic policy and debt management is very limited. Governments that overstep those margins, especially in the debt structures that they create, are inviting trouble, as witnessed by the current problems of Russia and Ukraine. Their debts were inappropriately structured. Short-term debt operations were successful in raising the finance needed to cover budget deficits early on, but the governments of Russia and Ukraine relied too heavily on these instruments. Both countries financed excessive budget deficits over unduly long periods of time in a way that proved unmanageable. The temptation to go out and use the new markets and tax new instruments rather than fundamentally correct the underlying budget problems resulted in the fall of the Kiriyenko government.

Lipton also argued that the problem is not open capital markets but rather how those markets are managed. It is the institutional underpinnings of the openness of the market and the incentives that are built into the system that are most important, not openness per se. The institutional underpinnings can be improved; policies to redress imbalances can be implemented differently, better, and correctly. This is what the international community needs to focus on, rather than simply coming to the rash conclusion that the opening of capital markets in and of itself is problematic.

It is true that the opportunities created by openness are often misused. Markets can be used (or misused) to make short-term gains. The misuse of markets is not unavoidable, and it is not the openness of markets that should be blamed. Prudence needs to be exercised by all those assessing the markets. Some prudence should be enforced in various ways, including through supervisory and regulatory mechanisms. Many countries are lacking in these areas and need assistance putting into place currency exposure limits, capital adequacy standards, and short-term exposure limits for banks.

International financial markets exacerbated the adjustment process because of the way in which local financial markets were opened and because of the failure of outside investors to act prudently. Investors put too much faith in fixed exchange rates. In this environment, a number of financial institutions sold exchange-rate contracts and other economic instruments to people who did not understand what they were buying.

The loss of liquidity in these markets is a significant problem, especially if some of the largest traders in international financial markets permanently withdraw from the affected regions, but it is not the key cause of the crisis. Weaknesses in domestic banking systems due to inappropriate investments and poorly matched assets and liabilities were the primary cause of the current crisis. However, a return of foreign investors to these markets would mitigate the downturn. Some analysts expected investors to quickly return to buy up stocks and other financial assets at lower prices. Such a return would help the problem correct itself. Unfortunately, investors have yet to return to these markets in force. They have been dissuaded by the ongoing price volatility in financial markets. Investors should remember that price volatility is a reflection of uncertainty, not a core part of the problem.

Investors also need to better appreciate the effects that a new policy implemented by a government will have on the domestic and international capital markets. In the case of Southeast Asia, the markets did not understand what might happen as exchange rates were floated. Instead, they operated as if the direction of policy had not changed because the markets were used to the former stability.

Although the benefits from the flow of international capital are enormous, openness must be dealt with in a way that minimizes the risk. This has important implications for national authorities, for supervisory regimes, and for international organizations working in this area. A set of institutional changes needs to be put into place for workouts because many companies are unlikely to open their balance sheets to show how bad the conditions in their various subsidiaries are. Instead, the authorities may want to present a list of options from which to choose, country by country. The process will require a great deal of interaction with and money from the private sector. A process of restructuring must begin; assets need to be structured in a form that can be bought and sold. Governments also need to carefully plan the proper sequence of steps that must precede the opening of capital markets, and they should exercise prudence in not moving too rapidly. Countries often fail to recognize the limits beyond which vulnerability can increase at a startling pace.

The International Monetary Fund

Lipton also argued that the IMF faces institutional and financial limits to what it can do. In general, it is very difficult for the IMF to go public about a member country's economic difficulties. The IMF, owned by its members and working closely with them, often does not believe that going public with its concerns about a country's problems would be useful. For example, the IMF's analysis was absolutely correct in the Thai case, but it did not feel comfortable making its misgivings public because by doing so, the IMF might precipitate the very crisis it was trying to prevent. The IMF encourages governments to do the things they need to do, and it simultaneously attempts to keep the government credible with creditors. Many countries use the IMF as a symbol of approval. The IMF also tries to emphasize the positive in a situation.

Lipton argued that is unrealistic to expect the IMF to be the principal whistle-blower concerning inappropriate economic policies. This job is more properly that of the rating agencies, who, in his view, failed to indicate the looming problems in Southeast Asia. Ratings agencies missed the risks associated with increased lending to these countries; they are now overreacting in a bid to compensate for being wrong before. The ratings agencies had clues that something was wrong. Institutions with substantial amounts of shareholder capital at stake were overexposed. And other groups missed the signals and acted inappropriately in Southeast Asia as well: Japanese banks without real capital, Korean banks, and German state-owned banks that should not have been lending to Asia.

One way to improve external monetary policy while avoiding public criticism by the IMF is to improve transparency. For many countries, transparency has already improved. Agreements are now posted on the World Wide Web, and financial arrangements between the IMF and member countries under Article IV are made public.

The European Union

In the EU, freer capital movements have been closely linked to other EU policies. The experience of emerging markets has demonstrated that the process of opening capital markets needed to be more gradual and to be accompanied by fiscal and monetary reforms. Even within the EU, a system of completely open capital flows was not created until the early 1990s. The subsequent improvements in efficiency have helped to create a single financial market.

Regarding emerging markets, financial markets need to have a strong-enough base to cope with large inflows. Financial information provided by banks must also be transparent. The main emphasis of policy in these countries must be to put significant reforms into place. Rushing to adopt capital controls may do more harm than good; the international financial community needs to carefully evaluate what tools to use. The main policy for emerging markets must be the creation of a framework for broad, open markets as determined in a country-by-country analysis. As shown by the EU's experience, the balance of costs and benefits from the liberalization of capital movements is likely to remain positive despite the experience of 1997–98.

United States

The crises demonstrate that the world is closely linked and that the economic health of the United States is clearly tied to the economic health of the world. Since some in Congress appear willing to allow the United States to stand back and let the crisis pass it by, others are concerned about a turn against globalization and openness. However, the risk of failing to respond is much more serious than just standing by. Data already show that U.S. exports are down and that the current account deficit may grow by 1 percentage point of GDP in 1998. The approval of full funding of $18 billion for the IMF by the U.S. Congress during budget negotiations demonstrates that the United States remains committed to its role as the leader within the global economic community, at least for now.

U.S. President Bill Clinton has stated that the United States should not retreat from its global interests. The United States hopes to achieve its goals by executing the following policies:

1. The United States must avoid a deflationary cycle like the one experienced in the 1920s and 1930s; to date, the United States has demonstrated a commitment to avoid deflation by following a strong economic policy.
2. The United States will continue to work with emerging economies and especially with members of the G-22, who met again at the end of October 1998 after working groups had met all summer and produced three working papers on global financial reform. The U.S. focus will be on making exchange-rate regimes more flexible, since maintaining too much rigidity for too long has clearly caused some problems. The United States believes that countries should find a way to exit from rigid regimes much more quickly. However, countries have also found that capital controls are very dangerous and should be resisted.
3. The strong deterioration in capital markets demonstrates the need for increased liquidity and higher reserves. The United States must help to guarantee that the IMF has the resources to handle the crisis. The administration wants to keep the IMF at the center of international financial dealings because of its human capital and resources.
4. In addition, the private sector has to play a role in overcoming this crisis. The U.S. government wants to look at how private funds can help other countries better weather or avoid economic contagion, because such crises will occur again. The U.S. government would like to learn whether there is a set of procedures that could make bailouts orderly, if possible.

Globalization has forced the United States to innovate and compete, but openness and integration need to continue because, in the view of the United States, this system has brought a number of benefits to the United States and to countries with emerging markets, despite the current setbacks.

Chapter 8

Is Financial Globalization Working?

In the final session of the conference, four panelists—Jeffrey Shafer, Managing Director, Salomon Smith Barney, New York; Jack Boorman, Director, Policy Development and Review, International Monetary Fund, Washington, D.C.; Keun-Yung Lee, Chief Representative, Bank of Korea, Washington, D.C.; and Werner Schule, Counselor for Economic and Financial Affairs, Delegation of the European Commission, Washington, D.C.—participated in a roundtable discussion: "Is Financial Globalization Working?" Most of the participants agreed that although the current economic crisis is global in scope, it is not a crisis of globalization. The participants argued that economic interlinkages have always existed; the current problems are not due to these links but were caused primarily by domestic instability. Lee added, however, that international financial markets have exacerbated some of the crises in Asia and in some cases triggered currency declines that might have been avoided. To prevent future crises, international financial organizations must learn how to exploit the efficiency gains that accrue from open international capital markets while they also limit instability in world financial markets in the process of financial globalization. However, the world financial market is presently not well prepared to solve this problem because it lacks the stabilization measures available to national financial markets. Therefore, the world financial market must be provided with the resources to facilitate stability in the midst of expanding globalization. To conclude, the panelists explored the progress to date of Southeast Asian countries in dealing with the crises, and they laid out steps that need to be taken by the Russian government. The roundtable concluded with a brief discussion of the repercussions for Latin America of the "Asian flu."

World Financial Markets

Financial globalization has evolved over time. International flows of goods and services will continue to grow in the future regardless of how globalization is defined. However, in recent years there have been several new developments. Technology has improved the efficiency of financial markets. Markets are more open, and rules and procedures have become standardized. There is more integration in the world financial market as increasing numbers of national financial markets have become more closely tied to the major world financial centers. The mobility of international capital is immense, and it moves around the world financial markets continuously, increasing the volatility of those markets. Over time, private capital flows have increased as official capital flows have receded.

The privatization of world capital markets has helped to more appropriately distribute capital. However, the markets are much more volatile than in the past, and no financial market or national economy is immune to economic shocks. A liquidity crisis can quickly spin into a full-blown economic crisis.

In globalization, stress and pain are not universal. Western Europe is enjoying the best economic conditions in a decade, and the economy of the United States also continues to exceed all expectations. Most significant, Poland and Hungary have avoided economic contagion because their current economic ties to Russia are not strong and both countries pursue market-oriented economic policies. China differs from the other Asian countries. Foreign trade as a share of GDP in China is much lower, capital controls are much stricter, and the economy is in an earlier stage of development, so the country is not as dependent on international markets for growth. Moreover, the Chinese government is attempting to forestall a crisis by shoring up the domestic banking system and pressuring enterprises to restructure.

The current problems in economies in crisis are caused by domestic vulnerabilities and policy mistakes. Banking systems and corporations in many countries largely operated without hard budget constraints. These economies were quite brittle and shattered easily under modest pressure. The world has always been interlinked, and the current tie-ups are not fundamentally different from those in the past. However, serious external problems have damaged domestic economies.

If the problem were globalization, countries that attempted to insulate themselves from international financial markets should have performed well. However, Korea tried very hard to isolate itself globally through strong capital controls. China has insulated itself through more draconian measures. Yet, both countries have been adversely affected by the Asian crisis.

The problem posed by the current push toward financial globalization is very basic in nature. International financial organizations must learn how to exploit the efficiency gains that accrue from open international capital markets while they also limit instability in world financial markets in the process of financial globalization. However, it would be fair to say that world financial markets are not presently well prepared to solve this problem effectively when faced with the growing possibility of world economic crises, despite the sincere efforts of the affected governments, central banks, the IMF, and other international institutions.

It is usually accepted that financial markets are different from other markets. Perceiving that instability in financial markets could jeopardize the whole economy of the country, a government may thus attempt to stabilize financial markets by using measures that are not employed in other markets. These stabilization programs usually include three components: short-term liquidity supplied by the central bank; bank supervision; and deposit insurance. Through these measures, the government, and hence all citizens, pay for financial stability.

The world financial market lacks the stabilization measures available to domestic markets. The IMF has not been given the political mandate and resources enjoyed by many domestic central banks. The world does not have a system for supervising world financial markets and their participants. The world also lacks an explicit insurance system for capital flows. The global financial market lacks adequate stabilization measures in an increasingly unstable financial environment.

Since it would be extremely difficult to create a world central bank to act with the authority provided to domestic central banks, the role of the IMF should be strengthened. The provision of a stronger political mandate and more financial resources for the IMF is a more realistic solution than the creation of a world central bank. In conjunction with the IMF, the countries of the world need to come together to create a world economic forum, which would provide consolidated supervision over economic policies and financial markets of individual countries.

The benefits of keeping markets open are enormous, but the challenges must be dealt with in a way that potentially distills the benefits and minimizes the risk. Although the speed at which globalization proceeds can be monitored, a halt to globalization would be unwise and largely impossible. The world financial market must be provided with the resources to facilitate stability in the midst of expanding globalization. At the same time, individual countries must be more careful in managing their financial situations. Financial systems cannot be reconstructed overnight; they have to be rebuilt over time. Countries cannot wait until every last structural reform is in place before opening their markets; they need to restructure their financial institutions as they open their markets.

Southeast Asia

Many of the Asian economies are suffering sharp drops in GDP, and Japan is mired in banking problems and long-term recession. The Asian crisis should not be thought of as cyclical but rather as a result of structural problems. The affected countries need to focus on restructuring. In fact, the course of recovery is clear, and it is easy to see what types of changes need to be implemented. The situation in Korea and Thailand has already improved a bit. In both countries, there has been some success in stabilizing exchange rates, fiscal policy has been eased to encourage growth, and work has been done to end "crony capitalism." Thailand has announced measures to introduce financial sector restructuring and bank recapitalization. Korea has begun banking reform as well.

The situation in Indonesia is much less certain. The country is in a better position following Suharto's departure from office. However, the political situation remains volatile. Student protests continue, and relations with the Chinese minority remain strained. Upcoming elections may also lead to increased instability.

Malaysia demonstrates another approach to tackling economic crisis. However, the capital controls it has imposed may be counterproductive as the country becomes less attractive to FDI. The recently instituted capital controls may also distract attention from the serious structural changes that are needed. As in Indonesia, the political situation in Malaysia remains quite volatile, possibly more volatile than in Indonesia because a change of government has yet to occur and the jailing of the former prime minister has proven very divisive.

The Japanese crisis is entirely homegrown. The problems are not related to globalization. Money flows only out of Japan. The Japanese financial system has been in distress for the past eight years, but there has been no move to address its problems.

The Southeast Asian economies are currently too focused on repairing their own economies to look beyond those problems. As a result, they are unable to link together regionally to reassure the world that economic conditions are improving.

Russia

The outlook for Russia is very grim. Although Russian financial markets remain relatively small, the repercussions from their collapse have caused much concern about emerging markets in general. Economic reform in Russia was incomplete, and the economic situation was always fragile. The Duma's great struggles over the budget demonstrated the unresolved battle between reformers and recalcitrant factions. Throughout the transition, borrowing abroad continued and helped to lead to the current problems. However, Russia's economic problems mounted in 1998. Continuing political instability, policy failures, the "Asian contagion," and slumping commodity prices, especially for energy products, all helped to force the August 1998 devaluation. Political problems held back the reformist Kiriyenko cabinet. Market skepticism grew despite a large IMF bailout package of funds. The move to devalue was very risky. Political breakdown quickly accompanied economic collapse. Even with a reformist government and a sympathetic parliament in place, Russia would still have serious economic problems. With the political situation, the crisis is clearly much more serious. Reform has become a dirty word.

What needs to be done in Russia?

1. The government and the central bank need to resist pressure to spend and lend. These institutions need to draft consistent fiscal and monetary policies, but the policies of the new government makes such a course unlikely.
2. A realistic plan must be devised to deal with current debt issues.
3. Russia needs to face the broader challenge of unfinished reform that would allow Russians to invest domestically rather than being forced to invest abroad.

On the bright side, the Russian government has a broad base of support for the first time during the transition. Now, a new problem arises: what will the new government accomplish with this support?

Chapter 9

Subsequent Events and Future Challenges

The Wilson Center conference in September 1998 occurred at a moment of great flux in the international economic and political situation. The default by Russia had occurred barely one month earlier. Persistent criticism of the IMF's handling of both the Russian situation and the Asian crisis had delayed and jeopardized U.S. congressional approval of required additional funding for the IMF. At the time of the conference, participants saw U.S. approval of IMF funding as a critical component of moving forward to abate the crisis.

Likewise, the stalemate in Japan regarding both the stimulus of the Japanese economy and the resolution of its banking system problems preoccupied conference participants, who generally viewed Japan as a necessary long-term source of investment capital in the Asian region. Uncertainty prevailed over the next steps in the recovery of Indonesia, Korea, and Thailand, including whether the IMF would have the resources or obtain the necessary policy reform commitments to provide needed financial resources to countries in crisis.

Globally, the fear of financial contagion was complicated by the political calendar. Both Brazil and Venezuela had upcoming elections that would be influenced by, and would influence, the course of financial events. Also on the calendar were the World Bank and the IMF regular annual meetings, which were to be held in early October 1998 and were to be a focal point of multilateral response to the global economic situation.

Subsequent Events

Since the conference, key events have tended toward a stabilization of the crisis, though without eliminating the threat of further economic dislocation in Southeast Asia, in Southeast Europe, or globally. Perhaps the most important stabilizing event was the U.S. congressional approval, with certain conditions, of the enhanced IMF funding, including both a quota increase and an expansion of the "New Arrangements to Borrow" (NAB) to respond to future crises. That measure was approved on October 19, 1998, as part of the omnibus appropriations measure that funds major portions of the U.S. Government Fiscal Year 1999 budget.

U.S. approval permitted the activation of the additional funding needed by the IMF and paved the way for a rapid set of IMF actions to assist both countries in crisis and those threatened by near-term difficulties.

The largest IMF action was the financial rescue package agreed to by the IMF and the Brazilian government on November 13. The package rivaled the Korean rescue package in size. A total of $41.5 billion was committed to Brazil over three years, with $37 billion to be made available within the first year. The IMF itself was to provide $18 billion of that sum, with the World Bank supplying $4.5 billion and the Inter-American Development Bank also adding $4.5 billion. Finally, a consortium of industrialized nations, including the United States, was to provide $14.5 billion through the Bank of International Settlements.

In return for this assistance, thought necessary to prevent a possible rapid deterioration in the Brazilian currency's value and in the condition of the country's financial system, the government of Brazil made financial reform and fiscal discipline commitments consistent with the approach generally taken by the IMF.

The IMF took pains to claim that its program would "spare basic social programs from the expenditure cuts that fiscal discipline requires," as IMF Managing Director Michel Camdessus announced on November 13, 1998. Nonetheless, the Brazilian reform program is, at its core, an austerity approach built around the elimination of its public-sector budget deficits. Brazil pledged to reform certain key spending programs, including its social security system, and to achieve growing budget surpluses for the next three years.

Politically, these commitments came amid Brazilian elections and predictably engendered domestic opposition. The Brazilian Congress initially accepted some of the reforms but rejected others. In January 1999, speculative pressure on the Brazilian currency and the depletion of Brazil's foreign reserves forced the government of Brazil to abandon its fixed exchange rate. This action came despite the view, shared by the Brazilian government, the IMF, and the U.S. Treasury, that maintaining the fixed exchange rate was the desired policy for Brazil.

After the Brazilian real was permitted to float, it depreciated some 30 percent in a matter of weeks, causing rising interest rates and requiring a total reworking of the IMF package for Brazil. The long-term success of the IMF rescue efforts in Brazil will depend on whether fiscal discipline reforms are enacted, whether exchange-rate and interest-rate policies can avoid causing a recession in Brazil, and ultimately whether market confidence in Brazil is restored.

In November 1998, the IMF also reached an agreement with Indonesia on the implementation of reforms that would permit further IMF funding for that country. Additionally, the IMF hailed the Korean reform program as a success story, with Korea in position to repay a portion of its IMF borrowings by the end of 1998. Russia, however, remained mired in political controversy and economic failure, with IMF negotiations in December 1998 failing to achieve agreements leading to an immediate restoration of IMF assistance.

Meanwhile, the multilateral efforts to craft new responses to financial crises continued. Even before U.S. congressional approval of the IMF funding increases, the annual World Bank and IMF meetings in Washington, D.C., in early October 1998 saw new commitments by both the World Bank and the IMF to providing the resources needed to stabilize the global economy. A meeting of the G-22 nations convened by the United States also produced a set of three working papers, which detailed the international financial community's evolving thinking regarding the prevention and management of financial crises.

In Japan, in November and December 1998, progress was made on the twin issues of stimulus of the budget and resolution of the bank system weakness. Although the verdict remains out on their ultimate success, the largest initiatives yet taken by the Japanese government to address those longstanding problems received cautious praise from analysts.

Future Challenges

The conference discussions disclosed a general consensus on key points concerning the management of national economies in this period of globalization, but they also revealed uncertainty and disagreement on other issues.

First, the general consensus is that developing economies need external capital to achieve growth and necessarily must face the discipline of the international capital markets to attract that capital. In this sense, the "Washington Consensus," which favors free capital flows and enhancement of cross-order investment, was broadly supported.

Nevertheless, anxiety has been heightened by the 1997–98 Asian crisis about occasional irrationality, whether exuberant or panicked, in the capital markets. The potential clearly exists for the unfair treatment of nations that have in fact largely complied with the stated requirements of sound fiscal and monetary management. In that sense, there is a new interest in a reexamination of the "Washington Consensus" to see whether there are methods of reducing the volatility of capital flows or curtailing market overreaction to events that may deny countries the capital they need and contribute to a regional or global contraction in trade and investment.

That concern over the potential for episodic currency and capital crises in specific nations to segue into global crises and a recessionary cycle also infuses much of the continuing criticism of the IMF. Conference participants were muted in their criticism of the IMF, but some voiced concerns over whether IMF austerity requirements had exacerbated the Korean crisis and whether the IMF's initial, tough response to the Indonesian banking sector weakness had contributed to the bank panic there.

It should be noted that subsequent to the conference, political events in Brazil and Venezuela have showcased the continuing popular opposition to the IMF's standard approach. Moreover, even the IMF's sister institution, the World Bank, in December 1998 issued a report and statements that were perceived as critical of the IMF's insistence on fiscal discipline, cuts in social programs, and high interest rates as a response to these financial crises.

Regarding the problem of weak financial institutions, general fidelity to the "Washington Consensus" still left conference participants anxious about how to properly sequence the opening of capital markets and the creation of the necessary regulatory regimes to ensure safe and sound financial systems. Here there are really two objectives. The first is to create and sustain a safe and sound, properly regulated domestic banking system. The weakness in domestic banking systems is now consistently cited as the hallmark of the 1997–99 crises, but the difficulty is precisely that such weak banking systems cannot be made strong overnight. Regulatory laws and practices must be put in place, and the private-sector capacity to adhere to best practices and standards must be developed. This all takes time and manpower.

In the meantime, the second consensus goal of opening capital markets and permitting cross-border investment flows poses risks as well as offers development rewards. Even for those who generally oppose limits on capital flows, the crisis has made it apparent that the nature and mix of capital inflows—whether long-term or short-term investments, whether debt or equity instruments—can severely influence a nation's financial stability. And since many countries plainly lack the regulatory ability or authority to prevent bank mismanagement or misallocated lending, the challenge remains to balance openness to external capital with the need to wisely manage its inflow and deployment.

As for exchange-rate management, that key element in economic policy remains an extremely difficult area for prescription. The actual cases most widely watched by conference participants were those of Hong Kong and the People's Republic of China. Conferees generally were not certain whether either effort to maintain fixed rates of exchange could succeed, but there was consensus on the likely damage that would flow from an abrupt shift in either policy or from a failure to maintain the values of those currencies. Other nations in Asia particularly fear a devaluation of the Chinese renmenbi, since this would have major competitive implications for the export products of virtually all other Asian nations.

The conferees' concern over U.S. approval of IMF funding highlights another issue that remains of major importance to the maintenance of global financial order. The ongoing efforts of Southeast Europe and Southeast Asia to achieve stable growth in part through attracting foreign capital, and the financial crisis that hit the global economy in 1997–98, suggest that more future crises will occur and that the magnitude of the financial resources needed in response will increase.

Former U.S. Treasury Under Secretary David Lipton made that point by stating that "even a fully funded IMF will be stressed" by the need for greater liquidity and greater financial reserves in the global financial system. That point seems validated already by the large size of commitments made and pending before and since the Wilson Center conference. The uncertainty about whether the large Brazilian package will even suffice amplifies the point.

The question remains whether the resources now committed by donor nations to the IMF, by the World Bank, and by other multilateral agencies will be sufficient to stem the crises that are foreseeable over the next two to three years. If not, there is clearly a corollary question about the political willingness of the donor community to provide additional resources. The reluctant approval by the U.S. Congress of IMF funding is the most visible, but not the only, example of such donor fatigue or recalcitrance.

Appendix A

Tables

TABLE 1
REAL GDP
(in Billion 1997 Dollars)

	1990	1991	1992	1993	1994	1995	1996	1997	1998	1999
Albania	5.2	3.7	3.5	3.8	4.1	4.5	4.9	4.6	4.9	5.2
Bulgaria	43.4	38.3	35.5	35.0	35.6	36.4	32.8	30.5	31.6	32.2
Croatia	47.6	37.6	33.2	30.5	32.3	34.5	36.5	38.9	40.0	40.5
Macedonia	7.6	7.0	6.5	5.9	5.8	5.7	5.8	5.8	6.1	5.9
Romania	87.5	76.2	69.5	70.6	73.3	78.6	81.7	76.3	70.8	69.3
Slovenia	25.7	23.4	22.1	22.7	23.9	24.9	25.8	27.0	28.0	28.9
Yugoslavia	57.9	51.2	36.8	25.5	26.2	27.8	29.4	31.7	32.1	N/A
Total—SE Europe	274.9	237.4	207.1	194.0	201.2	212.4	216.9	214.8	213.5	N/A
Hong Kong	116.4	122.2	129.7	137.7	145.2	152.1	158.9	167.3	158.8	155.0
Indonesia	150.8	160.5	171.0	183.4	197.2	213.4	230.0	241.3	204.8	194.0
Malaysia	61.5	66.8	72.0	78.0	85.1	93.1	101.1	108.9	101.6	101.0
Philippines	71.9	71.9	71.9	73.4	76.7	80.3	84.8	89.3	88.8	87.2
Singapore	58.5	62.7	66.7	73.6	81.3	88.3	94.4	101.8	102.6	100.0
South Korea	321.2	350.6	368.3	389.7	423.2	460.9	493.6	520.8	491.1	488.4
Thailand	117.6	127.7	138.0	149.6	162.9	177.1	188.4	187.7	171.7	167.8
Total—SE Asia	897.9	962.4	1,017.6	1,085.4	1,171.6	1,265.2	1,351.2	1,417.1	1,319.4	1,293.4

TABLE 2
NOMINAL GDP
(in Billion Dollars)

	1990	1991	1992	1993	1994	1995	1996	1997	1998	1999
Albania	1.9	0.7	0.7	1.2	2.0	2.4	2.7	2.3	3.1	3.2
Bulgaria	17.4	7.6	8.6	10.8	10.0	13.1	10.1	11.2	13.3	13.1
Croatia	24.4	16.8	9.9	11.7	14.2	18.1	19.1	20.0	21.3	20.1
Macedonia	2.4	2.2	1.9	2.5	3.4	4.5	4.4	3.7	3.5	3.5
Romania	38.3	28.8	19.6	26.4	29.9	35.5	35.0	37.7	36.0	29.8
Slovenia	17.4	12.7	12.5	12.7	14.4	18.7	18.9	18.2	19.5	19.4
Yugoslavia	N/A	N/A	N/A	N/A	12.9	19.6	13.8	15.8	12.2	N/A
Total—SE Europe	N/A	N/A	N/A	N/A	86.8	111.9	104.0	108.9	108.9	N/A
Hong Kong	74.8	86.1	100.6	116.0	131.1	140.9	154.1	173.6	166.5	145.7
Indonesia	114.4	128.2	139.1	158.0	177.8	201.2	227.4	215.0	98.8	122.2
Malaysia	42.8	48.1	58.0	64.2	72.5	87.3	99.3	98.5	70.8	76.0
Philippines	44.1	45.4	49.8	54.4	69.9	72.7	83.8	82.4	67.5	74.2
Singapore	37.5	43.6	49.7	58.3	71.0	85.2	92.7	96.3	84.2	83.4
South Korea	253.7	294.2	307.9	332.8	380.8	456.4	484.6	442.5	288.8	300.5
Thailand	86.9	98.4	111.7	145.2	144.5	168.4	185.0	153.9	119.9	120.0
Total—SE Asia	654.2	744.0	816.8	928.9	1,047.6	1,212.1	1,326.9	1,262.2	896.5	922.0

TABLE 3
GDP PER CAPITA
(in 1997 Dollars at Purchasing Power Parity Exchange Rates)

	1994	1995	1996	1997	1998	1999
Albania	1,295	1,390	1,501	1,329	1,428	1,497
Bulgaria	4,217	4,337	3,984	3,705	3,831	3,907
Croatia	6,792	7,225	7,957	8,328	8,527	8,629
Macedonia	2,975	2,910	2,906	2,936	3,036	2,945
Romania	3,225	3,461	3,616	3,385	3,145	3,086
Slovenia	12,040	12,542	12,957	13,582	14,142	14,726
Yugoslavia	2,491	2,634	2,780	2,968	3,000	N/A
Hong Kong	24,607	27,014	27,533	28,130	25,949	25,179
Indonesia	3,526	3,756	3,988	4,120	3,446	3,212
Malaysia	8,882	9,447	10,028	10,551	9,666	9,414
Philippines	2,441	2,499	2,581	2,667	2,600	2,501
Singapore	23,677	25,240	26,461	27,971	27,865	26,523
South Korea	13,041	14,064	14,908	15,577	14,560	14,349
Thailand	6,538	7,008	7,483	7,381	6,669	6,432

TABLE 4
GDP GROWTH
(as Percent)

	1990	1991	1992	1993	1994	1995	1996	1997	1998	1999
Albania	-10.0	-28.0	-7.2	9.6	9.4	8.9	9.1	-7.0	8.0	5.4
Bulgaria	-9.1	-11.7	-7.3	-1.5	1.8	2.4	-10.1	-6.9	3.5	2.1
Croatia	N/A	-21.1	-11.7	-8.0	5.9	6.8	6.0	6.5	2.5	1.4
Macedonia	-9.4	-7.0	-8.0	-9.1	-1.8	-1.2	0.7	1.5	4.0	-2.4
Romania	-5.6	-12.9	-8.8	1.5	3.9	7.1	4.1	-6.6	-7.3	-2.1
Slovenia	-4.7	-8.9	-5.5	2.8	5.3	4.1	3.5	4.6	3.9	3.0
Yugoslavia	-6.6	-11.6	-27.9	-30.8	2.5	6.1	5.8	7.6	1.5	N/A
Hong Kong	3.6	5.0	6.2	6.1	5.5	4.7	4.5	5.3	-5.1	-2.4
Indonesia	7.0	6.5	6.5	7.3	7.5	8.2	7.8	4.9	-15.1	-5.3
Malaysia	9.7	8.6	7.8	8.3	9.2	9.4	8.6	7.7	-6.7	-0.6
Philippines	3.0	-0.1	0.0	2.1	4.4	4.7	5.7	5.2	-0.5	-1.8
Singapore	9.0	7.3	6.3	10.4	10.4	8.7	6.9	7.8	0.8	-2.5
South Korea	9.5	9.1	5.1	5.8	8.6	8.9	7.1	5.5	-5.7	-0.6
Thailand	11.2	8.6	8.1	8.4	8.9	8.7	6.4	-0.4	-8.5	-2.3

TABLE 5
POPULATION AND EMPLOYMENT
(in Thousands)

	1990	1991	1992	1993	1994	1995	1996	1997	1998	1999
Albania										
Population	3,293	3,260	3,190	3,167	3,202	3,249	3,283	3,447	3,464	3,482
Unemployment Rate	9.5	8.9	27.9	29.0	19.6	16.9	12.4	15.2	18.0	18.2
Bulgaria										
Population	8,991	8,632	8,540	8,460	8,444	8,406	8,413	8,419	8,427	8,434
Unemployment Rate	1.6	10.5	13.2	16.3	14.1	11.4	11.1	13.4	12.6	13.0
Croatia										
Population	4,778	4,514	4,470	4,641	4,649	4,669	4,494	4,572	4,577	4,586
Unemployment Rate	9.3	14.9	17.2	16.8	16.7	16.7	17.9	17.5	17.4	18.3
Macedonia										
Population	2,028	2,039	2,056	2,066	1,946	1,966	1,983	1,992	2,002	2,014
Unemployment Rate	23.6	26.0	27.8	29.3	32.0	37.7	41.1	44.2	47.4	47.9
Romania										
Population	23,207	23,185	22,789	22,755	22,731	22,681	22,600	22,546	22,503	22,460
Unemployment Rate	N/A	3.0	8.2	10.4	10.9	9.5	6.6	8.8	10.3	12.3
Slovenia										
Population	1,998	2,002	1,996	1,991	1,989	1,988	1,991	1,987	1,983	1,960
Unemployment Rate	4.7	8.2	11.6	14.6	14.5	14.0	13.9	14.4	14.5	14.4
Yugoslavia										
Population	10,529	10,409	10,448	10,482	10,516	10,547	10,574	10,659	10,700	N/A
Unemployment Rate	19.7	21.4	22.8	23.1	23.1	24.6	26.1	25.5	27.2	N/A
Hong Kong										
Population	5,700	5,750	5,810	5,920	6,060	6,190	6,310	6,468	6,700	6,700
Unemployment Rate	1.3	1.8	2.0	2.0	1.9	3.5	2.6	2.3	5.9	5.2

Indonesia										
Population	17,9830	182,940	186,040	189,130	192,220	195,280	198,340	201,390	204,400	207,600
Unemployment Rate	2.5	2.6	2.7	2.8	4.4	N/A	4.2	N/A	N/A	N/A
Malaysia										
Population	17,760	18,330	18,760	19,210	19,660	20,110	21,200	21,700	22,100	22,500
Unemployment Rate	5.1	4.3	3.7	3.0	2.9	2.8	2.5	2.7	8.4	7.3
Philippines										
Population	61,480	63,690	65,340	66,980	68,620	70,270	71,900	73,190	74,700	76,250
Unemployment Rate	8.1	9.0	9.8	9.3	9.5	9.5	8.8	8.9	10.5	11.2
Singapore										
Population	3,090	3,180	3,260	3,360	3,470	3,610	3,740	3,740	3,804	3,868
Unemployment Rate	1.7	1.9	2.7	2.7	2.6	2.6	3.0	2.4	N/A	N/A
South Korea										
Population	42,870	43,300	43,740	44,190	44,640	45,090	45,510	45,990	46,404	46,822
Unemployment Rate	2.4	2.3	2.4	2.8	2.4	2.0	2.0	2.6	9.6	8.8
Thailand										
Population	55,840	56,570	57,290	58,010	58,710	59,400	60,000	60,600	61,448	62,200
Unemployment Rate	2.2	2.7	1.4	1.5	1.3	1.1	1.1	0.9	N/A	N/A

TABLE 6
AVERAGE CONSUMER PRICE INFLATION
(as Percent)

	1994	1995	1996	1997	1998	1999
Albania	22.6	7.8	12.7	25.4	15.0	8.5
Bulgaria	95.9	62.1	123.3	1,082.8	22.3	−0.4
Croatia	97.6	2.0	3.6	3.7	5.7	3.8
Macedonia	121.8	15.9	3.0	4.4	1.0	3.7
Romania	136.7	32.3	38.8	154.2	59.3	42.6
Slovenia	21.0	13.5	9.9	8.4	8.0	6.6
Yugoslavia	3.0	79.0	93.0	18.0	29.7	N/A
Hong Kong	8.6	9.2	6.3	6.5	6.7	6.7
Indonesia	8.5	9.4	8.0	6.7	57.6	37.7
Malaysia	3.7	3.5	3.5	2.7	5.3	5.9
Philippines	9.1	8.1	8.4	5.1	8.9	9.2
Singapore	3.0	1.8	1.3	2.0	−0.3	0.5
South Korea	6.3	4.4	5.0	4.4	7.5	0.6
Thailand	5.1	5.8	5.8	−20.8	8.1	0.5

TABLE 7
AVERAGE EXCHANGE RATES
(in FCU/Dollar)

	1990	1991	1992	1993	1994	1995	1996	1997	1998
Albanian lek	9.0	24.0	81.3	105.6	95.4	93.0	104.8	149.6	140.0
Bulgarian lev	2.6	17.9	23.3	27.6	54.2	67.2	177.9	1,681.9	1,760.4
Croatian kuna	N/A	N/A	0.3	3.6	6.0	5.2	5.4	6.2	6.4
Macedonian denar	11.3	19.7	509.1	23.6	43.3	37.9	40.0	49.8	54.5
Romanian leu	22.4	76.4	308.0	760.1	1,667.0	2,034.0	3,093.0	7,158.0	9,401.0
Slovenian tolar	N/A	27.6	81.3	113.2	128.8	118.5	135.4	159.7	166.1
Yugoslavian dinar	11.3	19.6	2,467.1	N/A	1.6	2.0	5.0	5.6	9.5
Hong Kong dollar	7.8	7.8	7.7	7.7	7.7	7.7	7.7	7.7	7.8
Indonesian rupiah	1,842.8	1,950.3	2,029.9	2,087.1	2,160.8	2,248.6	2,342.3	2,909.4	10,014.0
Malaysian ringgit	2.7	2.8	2.5	2.6	2.6	2.5	2.5	2.8	3.9
Philippine peso	24.3	27.5	25.5	27.1	26.4	25.7	26.2	29.5	40.9
Singapore dollar	1.8	1.7	1.6	1.6	1.5	1.4	1.4	1.7	1.7
South Korean won	707.8	733.4	788.4	808.1	778.7	774.7	844.2	1,695.0	1,204.0
Thai baht	25.1	25.5	25.4	25.4	25.0	25.1	25.3	31.4	41.4

TABLE 8
EXPORTS
(in Million Dollars)

	1990	1991	1992	1993	1994	1995	1996	1997	1998
Albania	322	52	70	112	141	205	229	167	221
Bulgaria	2,615	3,737	3,956	3,726	3,935	5,345	4,890	4,938	4,294
Croatia	4,020	3,292	4,597	3,904	4,260	4,633	4,512	4,171	4,541
Macedonia	1,113	1,095	1,199	1,055	1,068	1,204	1,147	1,201	1,322
Romania	5,775	4,266	4,363	4,892	6,151	7,910	8,084	8,429	8,290
Slovenia	4,118	3,874	6,681	6,083	6,830	8,350	8,370	8,407	9,095
Yugoslavia	4,651	4,704	2,539	N/A	N/A	N/A	1,842	2,367	2,528
Hong Kong	82,160	98,580	119,490	135,240	151,400	173,750	180,750	188,060	173,990
Indonesia	25,675	29,142	33,967	36,823	40,055	45,417	49,814	53,443	48,848
Malaysia	29,445	34,361	40,691	47,099	58,652	73,865	78,312	56,760	75,460
Philippines	8,681	8,793	9,736	11,724	13,252	17,519	20,409	25,135	29,496
Singapore	52,527	58,972	63,444	73,942	96,456	118,185	125,015	125,009	110,700
South Korea	65,016	71,870	76,632	82,236	96,013	125,058	129,715	136,164	132,313
Thailand	23,485	28,494	32,481	36,913	45,484	55,937	62,538	38,250	61,250

TABLE 9
IMPORTS
(in Million Dollars)

	1990	1991	1992	1993	1994	1995	1996	1997	1998
Albania	456	124	524	602	601	679	921	685	849
Bulgaria	3,372	3,769	4,169	4,612	3,952	5,224	4,703	4,559	4,624
Croatia	5,188	3,828	4,461	4,666	5,229	7,510	7,888	9,104	8,383
Macedonia	1,531	1,274	1,206	1,199	1,442	1,719	1,464	1,589	1,722
Romania	9,202	5,793	6,260	6,522	7,109	10,278	11,435	11,275	11,820
Slovenia	4,727	4,131	5,892	6,237	7,168	9,305	9,252	9,179	9,870
Yugoslavia	6,701	5,548	3,859	N/A	N/A	N/A	4,102	4,790	4,792
Hong Kong	82,490	100,240	123,410	138,650	161,840	192,750	198,550	208,620	184,500
Indonesia	21,837	25,869	27,280	28,328	31,983	40,630	42,929	41,694	39,700
Malaysia	29,250	36,664	39,821	45,610	59,414	77,601	78,413	56,700	60,080
Philippines	13,080	12,853	15,433	18,854	22,584	28,388	34,127	36,900	29,500
Singapore	60,583	66,100	72,149	85,160	102,394	124,395	131,335	132,412	102,300
South Korea	69,884	81,525	81,775	83,800	102,348	135,119	150,339	144,616	93,282
Thailand	33,623	37,652	40,698	46,012	54,736	70,148	67,933	40,720	48,350

$$\text{Table 10}$$
$$\text{Trade Balance}$$
$$\text{(in Percent of GDP)}$$

	1990	1991	1992	1993	1994	1995	1996	1997	1998
Albania	-7.2	-10.6	-69.3	-41.3	-23.4	-19.6	-25.8	-22.4	-20.6
Bulgaria	-4.3	-0.4	-2.5	-8.2	-0.2	0.9	1.8	3.4	-2.5
Croatia	-4.8	-3.2	1.4	-6.5	-6.8	-15.9	-17.7	-24.7	-18.0
Macedonia	-17.1	-8.1	-0.4	-5.7	-11.0	-11.5	-7.2	-10.4	-11.3
Romania	-9.0	-5.3	-9.7	-6.2	-3.2	-6.7	-9.6	-7.6	-9.8
Slovenia	-3.5	-2.0	6.3	-1.2	-2.3	-5.1	-4.7	-4.2	-4.0
Yugoslavia	N/A	N/A	N/A	N/A	N/A	N/A	-16.4	-15.4	-18.5
Hong Kong	-0.4	-1.9	-3.9	-2.9	-8.0	-13.5	-11.6	-11.8	-6.3
Indonesia	3.4	2.6	4.8	5.4	4.5	2.4	3.0	5.5	9.3
Malaysia	0.5	-4.8	1.5	2.3	-1.1	-4.3	-0.1	0.1	21.7
Philippines	-10.0	-8.9	-11.4	-13.1	-13.4	-14.9	-16.4	-14.3	0.0
Singapore	-21.5	-16.4	-17.5	-19.2	-8.4	-7.3	-6.8	-7.7	10.0
South Korea	-1.9	-3.3	-1.7	-0.5	-1.7	-2.2	-4.3	-1.9	13.5
Thailand	-11.7	-9.3	-7.4	-6.3	-6.4	-8.4	-2.9	-1.6	10.8

TABLE 11
CURRENT ACCOUNT BALANCE
(in Million Dollars)

	1990	1991	1992	1993	1994	1995	1996	1997	1998
Albania	−118	−168	−51	15	−157	−12	−107	−276	−372
Bulgaria	−1,152	−874	−1,136	−1,617	−32	−26	82	427	−274
Croatia	−593	−589	823	600	786	−1,283	−858	−2,434	−1,554
Macedonia	−409	−259	−19	−36	−158	−216	−288	−275	−289
Romania	−1,656	−1,012	−1,564	−1,174	−428	−1,774	−2,571	−2,499	−3,010
Slovenia	129	759	926	192	600	−23	39	37	−4
Yugoslavia	−512	−536	−935	N/A	N/A	N/A	−2,260	−2,423	−2,264
Hong Kong	N/A	N/A	N/A	N/A	1500	−4,900	−2,160	−6,130	530
Indonesia	−2,988	−4,260	−2,780	−216	−2,792	−6,431	−7,800	−5,000	4,400
Malaysia	−870	−4,183	−2,167	−2,991	−4,520	−7,362	−4,800	−5,000	9,200
Philippines	−2,965	−1,034	−1,000	−3,016	−2,950	−1,980	−3,953	−4,351	1,295
Singapore	3,119	4,918	5,958	4,272	11,453	14,361	14,723	15,099	17,611
South Korea	−2,003	−8,317	−3,944	990	−3,867	−8,507	−23,006	−8,167	40,152
Thailand	−7,281	−7,572	−6,304	−6,364	−8,086	−13,554	−14,692	−1,200	14,090

TABLE 12
CURRENT ACCOUNT BALANCE
(as Percent of GDP)

	1990	1991	1992	1993	1994	1995	1996	1997	1998
Albania	-6.3	-24.6	-7.7	1.3	-8.0	-0.5	-4.0	-11.9	-7.7
Bulgaria	-6.6	-11.5	-13.2	-15.0	-0.3	-0.2	0.8	3.8	-2.1
Croatia	-2.4	-3.5	8.3	5.1	5.5	-7.1	-4.5	-12.2	-7.3
Macedonia	-16.8	-11.8	-1.0	-1.4	-4.7	-4.8	-6.5	-7.4	-8.2
Romania	-4.3	-3.5	-8.0	-4.5	-1.4	-5.0	-7.3	-6.6	-8.4
Slovenia	0.8	6.0	7.4	1.5	4.2	-0.1	0.2	0.2	0.0
Yugoslavia	N/A	N/A	N/A	N/A	N/A	N/A	-16.4	-15.4	-18.5
Hong Kong	N/A	N/A	N/A	N/A	1.1	-3.5	-1.4	-3.5	0.3
Indonesia	-2.6	-3.3	-2.0	-0.1	-1.6	-3.2	-3.4	-2.3	4.5
Malaysia	-2.0	-8.7	-3.7	-4.7	-6.2	-8.4	-4.8	-5.1	13.0
Philippines	-6.7	-2.3	-2.0	-5.5	-4.2	-2.7	-4.7	-5.3	1.9
Singapore	8.3	11.3	12.0	7.3	16.1	16.9	15.9	15.7	20.9
South Korea	-0.8	-2.8	-1.3	0.3	-1.0	-1.9	-4.7	-1.8	13.9
Thailand	-8.4	-7.7	-5.6	-4.4	-5.6	-8.0	-7.9	-0.8	11.8

Appendix B

Agenda for the Conference "Crisis and Transition in Southeast Asia, Southeast Europe, and the Global Economy," September 17–18, 1998

Opening Addresses
Chair: John Lampe, former Director of East European Studies, Woodrow Wilson Center, and Chair of the Department of History, University of Maryland–College Park.
"The Southeast Asian Economic Crisis in International Perspective," William Becker, Professor of History, George Washington University, Washington, D.C.
"Southeast Europe's Economic Transition: Its International Impact," Franz-Lothar Altmann, Deputy Director, Sudost Institut, Munich, Germany

Session 1. The IMF and Economic Sovereignty: What's Left for National Governments?
Part 1. Central Banks, Currency Boards, and Conditionality
Chair: John Lampe, former Director of East European Studies, Woodrow Wilson Center, and Chair of the Department of History, University of Maryland–College Park.
Bulgaria: Roumen Avramov, Member, Bulgarian Central Bank Board; Center for Liberal Strategies, Sofia
Indonesia: Soedradjat Djiwandono, former Governor, Central Bank of Indonesia, Jakarta

Part 2. Exchange Rates: When to Fix and When to Float?
Chair: Samuel F. Wells, Jr., Deputy Director, Woodrow Wilson Center, Washington, D.C.
Hong Kong and China: Edgardo Barandiaran, Senior Economist for East Asia and the Pacific Region, World Bank
Hungary: Peter Bihari, Chief Economist, Budapest Bank, Budapest, Hungary

*Session 2. Creating Sound Banking Systems: Domestic Regulation and
    Foreign Competition*
Chair: Barry M. Hager, President, Hager Associates, Washington, D.C.
Slovenia: Franjo Stiblar, Chief Economist, Ljubljanska Banka, Ljubljana,
    Slovenia
Thailand: Ijaz Nabi, Lead Economist, East Asia and Pacific, World Bank,
    Washington, D.C.

Session 3. Foreign Investment as Solution and Problem
Chair: Barry M. Hager, President, Hager Associates, Washington, D.C.
Southeast Europe: Vladimir Gligorov, Professor, Vienna Institute for
    International Economic Studies, Vienna, Austria
Russia and Global Capital Flows: Jeffrey Anderson, Director, European
    Department, Institute of International Finance, Washington, D.C.
Germany: Franz-Lothar Altmann, Deputy Director, Sudost Institut,
    Munich, Germany
Japan: Susumu Awanohara, Nikko Research, Inc., Washington, D.C.

Session 4. Keynote Address
Chair: Samuel F. Wells, Jr., Deputy Director, Woodrow Wilson Center,
    Washington, D.C.
"Priorities of U.S. Policy and the Regional Role of International Finan-
    cial Institutions," David Lipton, former Under Secretary for Interna-
    tional Affairs, U.S. Treasury, Washington, D.C.

Session 5. Roundtable Discussion: "Is Financial Globalization Working?"
Jeffrey Shafer, Managing Director, Salomon Smith Barney, New York
Jack Boorman, Director, Policy Development and Review, International
    Monetary Fund, Washington, D.C.
Keun-Yung Lee, Chief Representative, Bank of Korea, Washington, D.C.
Werner Schule, Counselor for Economic and Financial Affairs, Delega-
    tion of the European Commission, Washington, D.C.
Rapporteur: Paul Tibbitts, PlanEcon, Inc., Washington, D.C.

Index

agriculture: in Southeast Asia, 29, 30, 33; in Southeast Europe, 11, 12, 14, 16, 19, 43
aid, foreign, 12, 13, 19–20, 44. See also IMF
Albania, 16; economic and political background of, 10, 11–12; economic indicators for, 1990–1999, 92–104; transition in, 12, 20, 26, 42, 44
Anwar Ibrahim, 30–31
Aquino, Corazon, 31
Argentina, 40, 51
"Asian Economic Miracle," 1. See also "tiger" economies
"Asian flu": origins and spread of, overviews of, 3–4, 37–40; recovery from, overview of, 83–84. See also Southeast Asia; specific issues

baht (Thailand), 33–34, 61–62, 63, 99
balance of payments: crisis of in Southeast Europe, 1, 13–14, 26–27, 44, 51. See also current accounts
balance of trade. See trade balances
banking crises: in Russia, 23, 40, 70; in Southeast Asia, 29–30, 33–34, 35, 37–39, 53–57, 62; in Southeast Europe, 1, 14, 23, 24, 25–26, 49, 66–67. See also currency crises and devaluations; foreign currency loans
banking restructuring: in Central Europe, 69–70; currency boards and, 48, 49, 52; infrastructure and regulation for, 5–7, 8, 9, 35–36, 55, 56, 77, 79, 83, 89; objectives of, 67; in Southeast Asia, 6, 34, 35–36, 54–56, 63–65; in Southeast Europe, 6, 24, 43, 44, 66–68
Bank of International Settlements, 87
bankruptcy, 7, 21, 33, 34, 64, 68. See also loss-making firms
barriers to entry, 21. See also trade barriers

Belgrade, Yugoslavia, 19
black and gray markets, 15, 20, 73
Boorman, Jack, 9, 81
Bosnia-Herzegovina, 20, 26; economic and political background of, 10, 11, 12–13; future prospects for, 42, 44, 72–73
Bosnian war, 1, 15, 19, 24, 43, 73
Brazil, 86, 87, 90
budget deficits, 8, 23–24, 87; in Central Europe, 59, 70, 71; in Russia, 8, 23, 40, 70, 76–77, 84–85; in Southeast Europe, 25–26, 43–44, 51, 67. See also fiscal management
budget surpluses: in Southeast Asia, 38. See also fiscal management
Bulgaria, 16, 20, 74; banking and currency crisis in, 5, 14, 23, 25–26, 49; currency board of, 5, 14, 26, 47–53; economic and political background of, 13–14; economic indicators for, 1990–1999, 92–104; transition in, 22, 25, 27, 42, 43, 44, 45, 50–51
Bulgarian National Bank, 47

Camdessus, Michel, 87
capital flows: in Hungary, 60; international management of, 8–9, 78, 80, 81; mix of short-term vs. long-term, 7, 41, 69, 70–72, 89; regulation and control of, need for, 4, 5–6, 7, 9, 36, 37–38, 41–42, 53, 71–72, 77–78, 88–89; restrictions on, self-imposed, 7, 15, 18, 69–71, 82, 84; risks and volatility of, 2, 4, 8–9, 36, 81; in Russia, 7, 40, 70; in Southeast Asia, 1, 2, 3–4, 5–6, 30, 33–35, 39, 53–56, 62, 75; in Southeast Europe, 14, 15, 18, 19, 20, 27–28, 43, 44, 52, 71, 74. See also foreign direct investments; portfolio capital

107